AMERICA'S PRISONS

OPPOSING

VIEWPOINTS®

Other Books of Related Interest

AMERICA'S PRISONS

OPPOSING

VIEWPOINTS®

Clare Hanrahan, *Book Editor*

Bonnie Szumski, *Publisher*
Helen Cothran, *Managing Editor*

OPPOSING
VIEWPOINTS®
SERIES

GREENHAVEN PRESS

An imprint of Thomson Gale, a part of The Thomson Corporation

THOMSON

GALE

Detroit • New York • San Francisco • San Diego • New Haven, Conn.
Waterville, Maine • London • Munich

THOMSON

GALE

3 9082 10254 4999

LIBRARY OF CONGRESS CATALOGING-IN-PUBLICATION DATA
America's prisons / Clare Hanrahan, book editor.
p. cm. — (Opposing viewpoints series)
Includes bibliographical references and index.
ISBN 0-7377-3344-6 (lib. bdg. : alk. paper) —
ISBN 0-7377-3345-4 (pbk. : alk. paper)
1. Prisons—United States. 2. Imprisonment—United States. 3. Prison administration—United States. I. Hanrahan, Clare. II. Opposing viewpoints series (Unnumbered)
HV9471.A486 2006
365'.973—dc22   2005052659

Printed in the United States of America

"Congress shall make no law...abridging the freedom of speech, or of the press."

First Amendment to the U.S. Constitution

The basic foundation of our democracy is the First Amendment guarantee of freedom of expression. The Opposing Viewpoints Series is dedicated to the concept of this basic freedom and the idea that it is more important to practice it than to enshrine it.

Contents

Why Consider Opposing Viewpoints?

"The only way in which a human being can make some approach to knowing the whole of a subject is by hearing what can be said about it by persons of every variety of opinion and studying all modes in which it can be looked at by every character of mind. No wise man ever acquired his wisdom in any mode but this."

John Stuart Mill

In our media-intensive culture it is not difficult to find differing opinions. Thousands of newspapers and magazines and dozens of radio and television talk shows resound with differing points of view. The difficulty lies in deciding which opinion to agree with and which "experts" seem the most credible. The more inundated we become with differing opinions and claims, the more essential it is to hone critical reading and thinking skills to evaluate these ideas. Opposing Viewpoints books address this problem directly by presenting stimulating debates that can be used to enhance and teach these skills. The varied opinions contained in each book examine many different aspects of a single issue. While examining these conveniently edited opposing views, readers can develop critical thinking skills such as the ability to compare and contrast authors' credibility, facts, argumentation styles, use of persuasive techniques, and other stylistic tools. In short, the Opposing Viewpoints Series is an ideal way to attain the higher-level thinking and reading skills so essential in a culture of diverse and contradictory opinions.

In addition to providing a tool for critical thinking, Opposing Viewpoints books challenge readers to question their own strongly held opinions and assumptions. Most people form their opinions on the basis of upbringing, peer pressure, and personal, cultural, or professional bias. By reading carefully balanced opposing views, readers must directly confront new ideas as well as the opinions of those with whom they disagree. This is not to simplistically argue that everyone who reads opposing views will—or should—change his or her opinion. Instead, the series enhances readers' understanding of their own views by encouraging confrontation with opposing ideas. Careful examination of others' views can lead to the readers' understanding of the logical inconsistencies in their own opinions, perspective on why they hold an opinion, and the consideration of the possibility that their opinion requires further evaluation.

Evaluating Other Opinions

To ensure that this type of examination occurs, Opposing Viewpoints books present all types of opinions. Prominent spokespeople on different sides of each issue as well as well-known professionals from many disciplines challenge the reader. An additional goal of the series is to provide a forum for other, less known, or even unpopular viewpoints. The opinion of an ordinary person who has had to make the decision to cut off life support from a terminally ill relative, for example, may be just as valuable and provide just as much insight as a medical ethicist's professional opinion. The editors have two additional purposes in including these less known views. One, the editors encourage readers to respect others' opinions—even when not enhanced by professional credibility. It is only by reading or listening to and objectively evaluating others' ideas that one can determine whether they are worthy of consideration. Two, the inclusion of such viewpoints encourages the important critical thinking skill of objectively evaluating an author's credentials and bias. This evaluation will illuminate an author's reasons for taking a particular stance on an issue and will aid in readers' evaluation of the author's ideas.

It is our hope that these books will give readers a deeper understanding of the issues debated and an appreciation of the complexity of even seemingly simple issues when good and honest people disagree. This awareness is particularly important in a democratic society such as ours in which people enter into public debate to determine the common good. Those with whom one disagrees should not be regarded as enemies but rather as people whose views deserve careful examination and may shed light on one's own.

Thomas Jefferson once said that "difference of opinion leads to inquiry, and inquiry to truth." Jefferson, a broadly educated man, argued that "if a nation expects to be ignorant and free . . . it expects what never was and never will be." As individuals and as a nation, it is imperative that we consider the opinions of others and examine them with skill and discernment. The Opposing Viewpoints Series is intended to help readers achieve this goal.

David L. Bender and Bruno Leone,
Founders

Introduction

"Certainly, those people who pose a danger to the community should be behind bars. But more than half of the prison population is sentenced for nonviolent crimes. Let's start with the 1 million nonviolent prisoners and implement programs that work."

—David R. Karp, sociology professor

"The 'nonviolent' prison population is indeed sizable, but it isn't harmless. . . . The [Justice Department's] data tell us that 95% had an arrest history before the arrest that led to their current imprisonment. On average they had 9.3 prior arrests and about a third of these had been for violent crimes. The fact is that a sizable proportion of criminals sentenced for nonviolent offenses like buying dope is, in fact, chronically violent."

—Dan Seligman, Forbes *columnist*

There are more people confined in U.S. prisons and jails than are imprisoned in any other country. According to the U.S. Department of Justice, Bureau of Justice Statistics, 1 in every 138 U.S. residents, as many as 2,131,180 persons, were in prison or jail at midyear 2004. More than half of these were imprisoned for nonviolent crimes. The incarceration of nonviolent criminals is the subject of heated debate. Supporters contend that nonviolent offenders have broken the law and must serve time as a consequence. These analysts assert that nonviolent offenders often have a history of criminal activities, and by incarcerating them, the justice system is thereby reducing crime. Critics argue that imprisoning nonviolent offenders costs too much and does nothing to improve public safety.

Those who support the incarceration of nonviolent offenders claim that criminals deserve such punishment. According to criminologist Steve Rayle, "Every society has had, and will continue to have, a segment of the population that will not conform to the laws, customs, and norms that have been established. For these people, there will always be a price to pay," the International Association of Chiefs of Police contends that both violent and nonviolent offenders should do prison time. The association recommends that "convicted non-violent offenders should serve sentences in low-security facilities, established and funded by the federal government, to free up space for violent criminal offenders." Most important, say supporters of the incarceration of nonviolent offenders, putting these criminals behind bars helps reduce crime. "No single law or policy is by itself responsible for today's low levels of violent crime," U.S. attorney general Alberto Gonzales concedes, but he argues that "multiple, independent studies of our criminal justice system confirm what our common sense tells us: increased incarceration means reduced crime." Moreover, many analysts point out that while imprisoned, these offenders—many of whom are addicted to drugs—can receive help they would not likely receive outside of prison. Criminologists who defend incarceration for the property and drug-related crimes that comprise the majority of nonviolent offenses point to prison-based drug treatment programs and faith-based prison initiatives that offer intervention and rehabilitation that can turn lives around.

However, the rising expense of incarceration in both financial and social costs, and especially the increasing number of nonviolent prisoners, is a matter of concern to many. Critics from within and without the criminal justice system challenge the practice of imprisoning over 1 million nonviolent offenders. According to the Re-Entry Policy Council in a 2005 report, the U.S. spends as much as $60 billion a year on the criminal justice system. Yet of the 650,000 people released each year from federal and state prisons, as many as 70 percent will commit new crimes within three years, the Council reports. "Trying to control crime by building more prisons is like trying to blow your nose with $20 bills: It works, but it's not a very good idea," comments Matthew Yglesias, writing for the *American Prospect Online*. Ed Schwartz, of the Institute for the Study of Civic Values, asks if "churning people in and out of our prisons" is the only effective way to insure that crime stays down. "If it is," he predicts, "then we can count on staggering budgets for the criminal justice system for years to come." Senator Sam Brownback claims that "we've got a broken corrections system." The Kansas Republican argues that "recidivism rates are too high and create too much of a financial burden on states without protecting public safety."

Indeed, many states are facing serious budget shortfalls due to correctional spending and are looking for alternatives to keep prison costs low yet still protect the public. Advocates for criminal justice reform are calling for community-based sentencing alternatives such as halfway houses, day-report centers, drug courts, and mental-health and substance-abuse treatment centers for nonviolent offenders. These are interventions that many believe could fill the gap between prison and traditional probation at far less cost to taxpayers. But it remains to be seen if the changes in public policy that such alternatives would require can satisfy the concerns of both prison critics and proponents of incarceration.

The debate over the incarceration of nonviolent offenders will likely continue. Any investigation into the practices of America's criminal justice system will reveal that there are no easy solutions to crime and no consensus on the justness and effectiveness of prisons. In *Opposing Viewpoints: America's Prisons*, many aspects of the U.S. prison system are examined in the following chapters: Do Prisons Protect Public Safety? Are Prisons Just? How Should Prisons Operate? Who Should Be Imprisoned? The authors present differing viewpoints on how the prison system can best meet the public safety needs of citizens while preserving the human rights and dignity of the incarcerated.

CHAPTER 1

Do Prisons Protect Public Safety?

Chapter Preface

Since the onset of the war on drugs in the early 1980s there has been a vast effort to control the distribution and use of illicit drugs. The longer prison sentences resulting from the 1984 Sentencing Reform Act, which established determinate sentencing, abolished parole, and dramatically reduced good time credits, together with mandatory minimum sentencing laws, have resulted in tremendous increases in the U.S. prison population. Drug convictions account for most of this unprecedented growth. While proponents of the war on drugs argue that the war protects public safety, critics charge that the war is costly and ineffective.

Many public policy officials throughout the country are concerned that prison overcrowding, which they say has resulted from the drug war, is dangerous. When nonviolent drug offenders are sentenced to prison, these critics contend, violent criminals are released from prison to make room for them, thereby endangering the public. The American Bar Association argues that "lengthy periods of incarceration should be reserved for offenders who pose the greatest danger to the community and who commit the most serious offenses." Many critics have called for alternatives to incarceration and shorter sentences for offenders involved in drug crimes. The tax savings, they argue, could be invested in drug treatment, job training, transitional housing, and education for nonviolent offenders, all of which would be more helpful in getting offenders free of drugs and crime than is incarceration.

In contrast, proponents of the drug war contend that enforcement of drug laws protects America's most vulnerable from the harms associated with illegal drugs. According to Jodi L. Avergun, chief of staff at the Drug Enforcement Administration, "The Department of Justice and other law enforcement agencies at all levels seek to protect the most vulnerable segments of our society from those drug traffickers and drug addicted individuals who exploit those individuals least able to protect themselves." She adds: "The Department of Justice is committed to vigorously prosecuting drug trafficking in all of its egregious forms. Prosecutions range from high-level internal drug traffickers to street-level predators who are tempting children or addicts with the lure of profit and the promise of intoxication." U.S. attorney Leonardo M. Rapadas claims that the drug war successfully addresses "the pervasive violence and harm to society that inevitably accompanies the market for illegal drugs." He criticizes alternatives to prison for drug law offenders. These policies have "failed to prevent crimes or promote safer streets in the past. They would fail again today," he contends.

In the following chapter various authors present their views on how well America's prisons promote public safety. Because the drug war is fueling prison growth, it is often at the center of such debates.

"Researchers have found that 15 crimes are committed for every person released from prison, and that 17 crimes are avoided for every person put into prison."

Prisons Protect the Public from Violent Crime

David B. Muhlhausen

David B. Muhlhausen is a senior policy analyst with the Heritage Foundation, a Washington, D.C.–based research and educational institute. Muhlhausen, a top expert in Washington on criminal justice programs, argues in the following viewpoint that the most important job of government is to provide for the public safety. He contends that the quadrupling of the American prison population in the past two decades has saved millions of people from becoming victims of violent crimes. Muhlhausen also argues that prison construction and operations must remain a priority of government despite public dislike for prison spending. America's prisons are needed to incarcerate the hard-core offenders who threaten public safety, he maintains.

As you read, consider the following questions:
1. What percentage of violent criminals returns to prison within three years, according to Muhlhausen?
2. Why does Muhlhausen advocate building more prisons?
3. How can states save criminal justice funds, in the author's opinion?

S igns can be found nationwide that what critics call America's "love affair" with incarcerating prisoners may be coming to an end.

The legislature of Washington state, which passed the nation's first three-strikes-you're-out law by popular initiative a decade ago, recently passed a series of laws weakening it. Kansas now orders first-time drug offenders to treatment rather than prison, provided they didn't commit a crime that involved violence. Michigan has dropped its lengthy mandatory-minimum sentences for drug offenders. Iowa, Missouri and Wisconsin have eased their "truth in sentencing" laws, which require inmates to serve nearly their entire sentences before being eligible for parole.

In the last year, 25 states have sought to reduce the burden on their budgets and their corrections systems by weakening mandatory-sentencing statutes, reforming post-release requirements and restoring parole. Those proposing these measures come from both sides of the political aisle and from every level of government. They include sheriffs and police chiefs, legislators and members of Congress, governors and prison executives.

No Leniency Deserved

But if Alan Elsner, an author who focuses on criminal-justice issues, was correct in a recent op-ed for *The Washington Post* that our "love affair" with incarcerating dangerous criminals is waning, those proposing the changes are going to find that breaking up is hard to do. Americans have come to rely on the criminal-justice system to keep hard-core offenders locked up, and they won't think it's worth it when—in the name of cost-cutting—rapes, murders and other violent crimes go up by the thousands as a result of any veiled efforts to extend leniency to offenders who clearly don't deserve it.

The American people understand their state governments are in financial crisis and that the federal government expects record deficits in the near future. They sense that locking up some prisoners—first-time drug offenders, for instance—may be draining state money needlessly. The increased emphasis on rehabilitating prisoners and easing their return to society that President [George W.] Bush advocated in his [2005] State of the Union speech makes sense to many of them.

But they also know that the strengthening of sentencing laws in the early 1990s, the prison-building boom that began in that decade and efforts by prosecutors and lawmakers to take dangerous criminals off the street and keep them off has paid handsome dividends.

Ramirez. © 1997 by Copley News Service. Reproduced by permission.

The prison population in America has quadrupled since 1980 to more than 2 million people. Crime rates during the decade dropped to all-time lows. Coincidence? Consider that researchers have found that 15 crimes are committed for every person released from prison, and that 17 crimes are avoided for every person put into prison. The prison population in America has quadrupled since 1980 to more than 2 million people. Crime rates during the decade dropped to all-time lows. Coincidence? Consider that researchers have found that 15 crimes are committed for every person released from prison, and that 17 crimes are avoided for every person put into prison. Also along those lines, a 10 percent increase in prison population leads to a 13 percent decrease in homicides.

Considering that half the people in America's prisons are serving time for violent crimes, that means that, conservatively, millions of people have avoided becoming victims of such crimes thanks to these policies.

Harsh Penalties, Less Crime

Our society's increasing freedom from crime is the result of better law enforcement and harsher penalties. Reduce enforcement or relax the penalties, and we will likely find ourselves again up to our eyeballs in crime. . . .

Those who engage in criminal acts of violence have often been involved in hundreds of incidents before being arrested for the first time. Prison is the only way to protect the public from further criminal activity.

Edward I. Koch "Harsh Punishments Curb Crime," Newsmax.com, April 28, 2005. www.newsmax.com.

So pardon them if they're not quick to slash corrections budgets when corrections makes up so small a part of states' operational expenditures—about 6.7 percent, according to the latest research. Pardon their skepticism of a rehabilitation system with a long, miserable record of failure—two-thirds of those released from prison this year will be re-arrested within three years and almost 49 percent of the violent criminals released will return to prison in that time period.

Public Safety: Government's First Job

There is a lot of discussion in the country these days about the proper role and size of government. But all agree that providing for the public safety is its first and foremost job.

Right now, that means operating and building prisons will remain for some time to come a significant priority of government. America's state prisons operate today at up to 117 percent capacity, which means two things: we must ensure we incarcerate only those who truly should be in prison, and we must face the fact that we need more prisons, not fewer.

States can save money by more effectively prioritizing within their criminal-justice systems. They can find alternatives for first-time drug offenders and others who haven't committed violent crimes. They can bolster vocational training, which shows some promise of better preparing prisoners to find employment after release.

But there's only so much that can be done. America faced a real problem when the prison-building and sentence-strengthening movements began—a wave of violent crime that left much of the nation gripped in fear. This problem got better in the 1990s, but it hasn't gone away. And even if we can decrease recidivism, those who commit crimes, especially violent crimes, owe a debt to society and need to do their time.

In truth, America does not love prisons. We'd far rather neither have nor need them. But some of us clearly need to be in prison for the safety of the rest of us. As long as that's the case, we can, will and, indeed, must spend the money to do what it takes to incarcerate those people. Which means that breaking up with the tough law enforcement of the 1990s will indeed be hard to do.

"If the goal of our criminal justice system is to keep people safer and communities stronger, it is failing. Prisons are a very expensive revolving door. We imprison many, and spend a great amount of money doing it, and then welcome them right back in."

Prisons Increase Violence

Carolina Cordero Dyer

Carolina Cordero Dyer is the associate executive director of the Osborne Association, an organization working to promote a more effective and efficient criminal justice system and a safer and more just society. In this viewpoint Dyer asserts that the criminal justice system does not make Americans safer. Imprisonment undermines future work prospects for many of the 600,000 prisoners released each year, she asserts. This reduces the chance that they will become productive citizens and increases the likelihood of them engaging in more crime and ultimately returning to prison.

As you read, consider the following questions:

1. According to the author, how many people are locked up in the United States each year?
2. How much does it cost New York City to detain a juvenile for one year? How much for one year in a public high school, according to Dyer?
3. How can transitional and employment services for former prisoners be funded, according to the author?

Carolina Cordero Dyer, "Tough on Crime or Smart on Crime: Jobs Not Just Jails Make Our Streets Safer," www.realcostofprisons.org, April 27, 2005. Copyright © 2003 by the Drum Major Institute for Public Policy. All rights reserved. Reproduced by permission.

The United States locks up two million people each year, while another 4.6 million are under criminal justice supervision (parole or probation). Most of those involved in our criminal justice system have been convicted of nonviolent offenses; many for drug charges. A quarter of the entire world's prisoners are locked up in this country, although the United States represents only five per cent of the world's population. In fact, the United States has a higher rate of incarceration than any country in the world including Russia, Iraq, Iran, North Korea, and Indonesia.

Our philosophy of locking people up and throwing away the key has clearly not worked. Sentences in the United States are exceedingly long: five to six times those in Western Europe and Canada. Yet, recidivism remains high. Nationally, 51% of people released from prison return within three years. In New York, it's worse: two out of three will return within three years. And, studies demonstrate that a longer prison term doesn't make someone less likely to get arrested again.

In spite of all our tough-on-crime rhetoric in New York, most people that we lock up come home. Across the country, more than 600,000 inmates were released into society [in 2004]. New York State released 32,000, and 78% of them returned to New York City. In the same period, the New York State Division of Parole had more than 70,000 former prisoners under supervision, the vast majority of whom resided in New York City. In addition, more than 130,000 New Yorkers cycle through New York City's lock ups and jails each year.

All this doesn't come cheap. New York spends $32,000 annually to lock someone up in a state facility; $64,000 in a city jail. In New York City, we spend $9,739 to educate a young person in a public high school each year, but $131,000 a year to detain a juvenile in a facility. In a public budget climate of looming deficits of a magnitude we have never seen, incarceration dollars squeeze City and State budgets, taking essential dollars away from health care, education, care for the elderly, and other hallmarks of a civilized society.

If the goal of our criminal justice system is to keep people safer and communities stronger, it is failing. Prisons are a very expensive revolving door. We imprison many, and spend a great amount of money doing it, and then welcome them right back in. They don't become productive citizens, and there are more victims of crime, not fewer. If we want to keep our streets safer, we need to pay as much attention to what keeps pushing people through that jail door, as we do to what happens when they get out. . . .

Employing People with Criminal Records Benefits Society

It saves money, a concern that is more important than ever before. For every 500 people with criminal records employed in lieu of receiving welfare, a minimum of $4 million is saved annually. For every 500 people employed in lieu of returning to prison, $15 million is saved. Employed people are less likely to commit crimes and return to prison, thereby enhancing public safety. Prisoners return to communities already plagued by high levels of unemployment, poor public schools, and families ripped apart by the impact of crime and incarceration. Providing jobs to returning ex-offenders helps build communities instead of putting even more pressure on fragile neighborhoods. . . . Inmates released from a New York State facility typically receive $40 and a bus ticket to the Port Authority. The lucky ones have families or friends who will take them in. Many others find their way to the City shelter system—unemployed and homeless. Finding a decent job that pays a living wage is very hard for someone with a prison record. The challenges come from both the set-up for failure that the prison experience itself creates as well as the roadblocks that government policies have created.

Imprisonment undermines an individual's future work prospects. While prisoners hold "jobs," these jobs do not prepare them for work in the real economy. Typically, prison jobs teach inmates to work "dumber" by splitting one job into several small jobs. Nor are there consequences for doing a prison job slowly or poorly. No reward is given for creativity or initiative, and certainly none for teamwork, a concept that makes corrections officers uneasy. An inmate who has adapted well to prison has not been primed for a job in the community. Behavior learned in prison to survive—toughness, "attitude", and isolation—is the exact opposite of what is needed to be successful on the outside.

The restrictions that prisons impose on an adult's independence, spontaneity, and self confidence are internalized over time. After years in a crowded and confined environment, a prisoner reacts to the world's ordinary stresses with despair, hypersensitivity to disrespect, and alternating fearfulness and anger. The regimentation of prison life can erode a person's capacity to plan an orderly day, navigate the subways, make it to an appointment on time, or respond flexibly to the smallest of stumbling blocks. Because they lack usable work experience, many are pessimistic about their prospects for finding employment upon release. This pessimism expresses itself in many ways. Some ignore the future and refuse to make plans for employment. Others make plans that are unrealistic or require illegal behavior.

Prisons Are "Crime Factories"

Instead of curbing criminal tendencies, prisons encourage them. Violent and aggressive behavior is standard and even rewarded. It's clear that time served in such conditions regularly creates violent criminals from nonviolent ones.

Recidivism rates are exceedingly high. According to the Bureau of Justice Statistics, more than two-thirds of released prisoners are re-arrested within three years. These figures underline the ineffectiveness of prison as a deterrent and a reformer.

Rebecca Tuhus-Dubrow, *The Nation*, December 19, 2003.

When released, the former prisoner enters the job market yards short of the starting line. Eight in ten have a history of substance abuse, and many are sober for the first time in their lives. Many have never been employed outside of prison. The majority of those returning to New York City do not have a high school diploma. Many have poor critical thinking skills and cannot read. . . .

Further, former prisoners carry an additional disadvantage that shows itself every time he encounters an employment application's unforgiving question: Have you ever been convicted of a crime? In addition to fears and prejudice on the part of employers, many are restricted from certain types of employment, including caring for the elderly, airline security, healthcare, and plumbing.

Improving the System

How do we change the system to increase the chances of ex-prisoners finding the jobs that can keep them from repeating their crimes?

- Prisons and jails should provide realistic job training programs to every inmate, giving them skills that are marketable when they get out. At a minimum, require all prisoners to get a GED while incarcerated and provide the capacity for them to do so.
- Expand the use of community supervision, including work release and parole. It is ironic that politicians proclaim that ending parole or restricting work release enhances public safety. On the contrary, these programs serve as an important bridge between confinement and an independent, productive life on the outside. . . .
- Provide a continuity of pre- and post-release services. . . .
- New and expanded employment programs should combine work and job skills development to meet the immediate need for income and the longer-term need for skills and relationships. . . .
- Remove employment restrictions. At least six states bar ex-prisoners from public employment, and many state licensing agencies bar former prisoners from professions such as the law, real estate, medicine, nursing, teaching, physical therapy, and even, barbering. . . .

And, finally, we need to invest far greater government resources on transitional and employment services for people coming out of prisons and jails.

And, here is the surprising part: there is plenty of money available for this. The funds are available in state prison budgets but are being spent on ineffective strategies: locking too many people up, for far too long, based on far too arbitrary sentencing guidelines. Mandatory sentencing laws, such as the Rockefeller Drug Laws and Second Felony Offender laws in New York, should be repealed. Reform of the Rockefeller Drug Law, something the State of New York has been unable to do since 1973, could save $610 million annually if we provided alternatives to incarceration to just 19,000 drug offenders. The price of building the prisons to house those drug offenders saves another two billion dollars in capital costs.

Politicians must stop pandering to the public's fears. Tough on crime, the war on drugs, three strikes—these are all empty sound bites that have led prosecutors to seek longer and longer sentences, legislatures to lengthen sentences in order to cure every societal ill, led to criminalizing more behavior, led to the incarceration of our young people, led to the demonization of prisoners and former prisoners, led to the devastation of families and communities, and led to barriers to employment for those who have served their time.

The irony of it all is that so much of what we have done to contribute to this mess has been done in the name of public safety. But to ignore the needs of the 600,000 returning to society does not make our streets safer. It is instead extraordinarily costly, increases the likelihood that new crimes will be committed, and puts further strain on fragile communities.

We can do better and we must do better. We must shift our thinking about crime and punishment and turn our focus to crime prevention; addressing the root causes of crime such as lack of employment; and devoting our resources to community building, education, and workforce development that provides jobs at a living wage. The future of our communities and our society depends upon it.

"The notion that harsh drug laws are to blame for filling prisons to the bursting point . . . appears to be dubious."

Imprisoning Drug Offenders Makes America Safer

James R. McDonough

James R. McDonough, the director of the Florida Office of Drug Control, argues in this viewpoint that many drug felons are also perpetrators of other crimes. Drugs drive crime, the author contends, and he points out that many drug felons have extensive arrest histories for offenses including burglary and prostitution, and for violent crimes, such as armed robbery and aggravated assault. By incarcerating drug offenders, McDonough contends, law enforcement is making Americans safer.

As you read, consider the following questions:

1. What criminal charges in addition to possession are associated with drug offenses, in McDonough's view?
2. Which illicit drug is most often associated with an extensive history of prior arrests, according to the author?
3. What misbehaviors, according to McDonough, accompany marijuana use among youth ages 12 to 17?

An oft-repeated mantra of both the liberal left and the far right is that antidrug laws do greater harm to society than illicit drugs. To defend this claim, they cite high rates of incarceration in the United States compared with more drug-tolerant societies. In this bumper-sticker vernacular, the drug war in the United States has created an "incarceration nation." But is it true? Certainly rates of incarceration in the United States are up (and crime is down). Do harsh antidrug laws drive up the numbers? Are the laws causing more harm than the drugs themselves? These are questions worth exploring, especially if their presumptive outcome is to change policy by, say, decriminalizing drug use.

It is, after all, an end to the "drug war" that both the left and the right say they want. For example, William F. Buckley Jr. devoted the Feb. 26, 1996, issue of his conservative journal, *National Review*, to "the war on drugs," announcing that it was lost and bemoaning the overcrowding in state prisons, "notwithstanding that the national increase in prison space is threefold since we decided to wage hard war on drugs." James Gray, a California judge who speaks often on behalf of drug-decriminalization movements, devoted a major section of his book, *Why Our Drug Laws Have Failed and What We Can Do About It*, to what he calls the "prison-industrial complex." Ethan Nadelmann, executive director of the Drug Policy Alliance and perhaps the most unabashed of the "incarceration-nation" drumbeaters, says in his Web article, "Eroding Hope for a Kinder, Gentler Drug Policy," that he believes "criminal-justice measures to control drug use are mostly ineffective, counterproductive and unethical" and that administration "policies are really about punishing people for the sin of drug use." Nadelmann goes on to attack the drug-court system as well, which offers treatment in lieu of incarceration, as too coercive since it uses the threat of the criminal-justice system as an inducement to stay the course on treatment.

Bad Drug Laws Do Not Fill Prisons

In essence, the advocates of decriminalization of illegal drug use assert that incarceration rates are increasing because of bad drug laws resulting from an inane drug war, most of whose victims otherwise are well-behaved citizens who happen to use illegal drugs. But that infraction alone, they say, has led directly to their arrest, prosecution and imprisonment, thereby attacking the public purse by fostering growth of the prison population. Almost constant repetition of such assertions, unanswered by voices challenging their validity, has resulted in the decriminalizers gaining many converts. This in turn has begotten yet stronger assertions: the drug war is racist (because the prison population is overrepresentative of minorities); major illegal drugs are benign (ecstasy is "therapeutic," "medical" marijuana is a "wonder" drug, etc.); policies are polarized as "either-or" options ("treatment not criminalization") instead of a search for balance between demand reduction and other law-enforcement programs; harm reduction (read: needle distribution, heroin-shooting "clinics," "safe drug-use" brochures, etc.) becomes the only "responsible" public policy on drugs. But the central assertion, that drug laws are driving high prison populations, begins to break down upon closer scrutiny. Consider these numbers from the U.S. Bureau of Justice Statistics compilation, Felony Sentences in State Courts, 2000. Across the United States, state courts convicted about 924,700 adults of a felony in 2000. About one-third of these (34.6 percent) were drug offenders. Of the total number of convicted felons for all charges, about one-third (32 percent) went straight to probation. Some of these were rearrested for subsequent violations, as were other probationers from past years. In the end, 1,195,714 offenders entered state correctional facilities in 2000 for all categories of felonies. Of that number, 21 percent were drug offenders. Seventy-nine percent were imprisoned for other crimes.

Therefore, about one-fifth of those entering state prisons in 2000 were there for drug offenses. But drug offenses comprise a category consisting of several different charges, of which possession is but one. Also included are trafficking, delivery and manufacturing. Of those incarcerated for drug offenses only about one-fourth (27 percent) were convicted of possession. One-fourth of one-fifth is 5 percent. Of that small amount, 13 percent were incarcerated for marijuana possession, meaning that in the end less than 1 percent (0.73

percent to be exact) of all those incarcerated in state-level facilities were there for marijuana possession. The data are similar in state after state. At the high end, the rates stay under 2 percent. Alabama's rate, for example, was 1.72 percent. At the low end, it falls under one-tenth of 1 percent. Maryland's rate, for example, was 0.08 percent. The rate among federal prisoners is 0.27 percent. If we consider cocaine possession, the rates of incarceration also remain low—2.75 percent for state inmates, 0.34 percent for federal. The data, in short, present a far different picture from the one projected by drug critics such as Nadelmann, who decries the wanton imprisonment of people whose offense is only the "sin of drug use."

Prison Drug Treatment Works

The therapeutic community model of prison substance abuse treatment and aftercare has been implemented in state and federal prisons across the country, significantly reducing recidivism rates.

In its 2002 Annual Report to Congress on substance abuse treatment programs in the nation's federal prisons, the Federal Bureau of Prisons reports that 50 of the Bureau's prisons have a residential drug abuse treatment program in which inmates are housed together in a separate unit of the prison that is reserved for drug abuse treatment as they were in Wexler's California prison study. In fiscal year 2002, more than 16,000 inmates participated in the in-prison residential drug abuse treatment programs and more than 13,000 participated in community transition drug abuse treatment. Rigorous analysis of these programs by the Bureau of Prisons and the National Institute on Drug Abuse shows these programs make a significant positive difference in the lives of inmates following their release from prison as they were substantially less likely to use drugs or be rearrested compared to other inmates who did not participate in the treatment programs.

Bureau of Prisons, 2003.

But what of those who are behind bars for possession? Are they not otherwise productive and contributing citizens whose only offense was smoking a joint? If Florida's data are reflective of the other states—and there is no reason why they should not be—the answer is no. In early 2003, Florida had a total of 88 inmates in state prison for possession of marijuana out of an overall population of 75,236 (0.12 percent). And of those 88, 40 (45 percent) had been in prison before. Of the remaining 48 who were in prison for the first time, 43 (90 percent) had prior probation sentences and the probation of all but four of them had been revoked at least once. Similar profiles appear for those in Florida prisons for cocaine possession (3.2 percent of the prison population in early 2003). They typically have extensive arrest histories for offenses ranging from burglary and prostitution to violent crimes such as armed robbery, sexual battery and aggravated assault. The overwhelming majority (70.2 percent) had been in prison before. Of those who had not been imprisoned previously, 90 percent had prior probation sentences and the supervision of 96 percent had been revoked at least once.

The notion that harsh drug laws are to blame for filling prisons to the bursting point . . . appears to be dubious. Simultaneously, the proposition that drug laws do more harm than illegal drugs themselves falls into disarray even if we restrict our examination to the realm of drugs and crime, overlooking the extensive damage drug use causes to public health, family cohesion, the workplace and the community.

Illicit Drug Use Drives Crime

Law-enforcement officers routinely report that the majority (i.e., between 60 and 80 percent) of crime stems from a relationship to substance abuse, a view that the bulk of crimes are committed by people who are high, seeking ways to obtain money to get high or both. These observations are supported by the data. The national Arrests and Drug Abuse Monitoring (ADAM) program reports on drugs present in arrestees at the time of their arrest in various urban areas around the country. In 2000, more than 70 percent of people arrested in Atlanta had drugs in their system; 80 percent in New York City; 75 percent in Chicago; and so on. For all cities measured, the median was 64.2 percent. The results are equally disturbing for cocaine use alone, according to Department of Justice Statistics for 2000. In Atlanta, 49 percent of those arrested tested positive for cocaine; in New York City, 49 percent; in Chicago, 37 percent. Moreover, more than one-fifth of all arrestees reviewed in 35 cities around the nation had more than one drug in their bodies at the time of their arrest, according to the National Household Survey on Drug Abuse.

If the correlation between drug use and criminality is high for adults, the correlation between drug use and misbehavior among youth is equally high. For children ages 12 to 17, delinquency and marijuana use show a proportional relationship. The greater the frequency of marijuana use, the greater the incidents of cutting class, stealing, physically attacking others and destroying other peoples' property. A youth who smoked marijuana six times in the last year was twice as likely physically to attack someone else than one who didn't smoke marijuana at all. A child who smoked marijuana six times a month in the last year was five times as likely to assault another than a child who did not smoke marijuana. Both delinquent and aggressive antisocial behavior were linked to marijuana use—the more marijuana, the worse the behavior.

Even more tragic is the suffering caused children by substance abuse within their families. A survey of state child-welfare agencies by the National Committee to Prevent Child Abuse found substance abuse to be one of the top two problems exhibited by 81 percent of families reported for child maltreatment. Additional research found that chemical dependence is present in one-half of the families involved in the child-welfare system. In a report entitled No Safe Haven: Children of Substance-Abusing Parents, the National Center on Addiction and Substance Abuse at Columbia University estimates that substance abuse causes or contributes to seven of 10 cases of child maltreatment and puts the federal, state and local bill for dealing with it at $10 billion.

Are the drug laws, therefore, the root of a burgeoning prison population? And are the drug laws themselves a greater evil than the drugs themselves? The answer to the first question is a clear no. When we restricted our review to incarcerated felons, we found only about one-fifth of them were in prison for crimes related to drug laws. And even the minuscule proportion that were behind bars for possession seemed to have serious criminal records that indicate criminal behavior well beyond the possession charge for which they may have plea-bargained, and it is noteworthy that 95 percent of all convicted felons in state courts in 2000 pleaded guilty, according to the Bureau of Justice Statistics.

The answer to the second question also is no. Looking only at crime and drugs, it is apparent that drugs drive crime. While it is true that no traffickers, dealers or manufacturers of drugs would be arrested if all drugs were legal, the same could be said of drunk drivers if drunken driving were legalized. Indeed, we could bring prison population down to zero if there were no laws at all. But we do have laws, and for good reason. When we look beyond the crime driven by drugs and factor in the lost human potential, the family tragedies, massive health costs, business losses and neighborhood blights instigated by drug use, it is clear that the greater harm is in the drugs themselves, not in the laws that curtail their use.

| "*Criminal justice measures to control drug use are mostly ineffective, counterproductive and unethical, and should generally be used as last, not first resorts.*"

Imprisoning Drug Offenders Does Not Make America Safer

Ethan Nadelmann

Ethan Nadelmann is the founding director of the Drug Policy Alliance, a leading organization promoting alternatives to the war on drugs. In this viewpoint Nadelmann argues that the criminal justice system should be employed as the last resort in efforts to control drug abuse and the crime that attends it. He contends that locking up drug users and then forcing them to undergo drug treatment as a condition of release is inconsistent with good drug treatment policies. Indeed, many abusers forced to undergo treatment relapse, he asserts.

As you read, consider the following questions:
1. What is Nadelmann's opinion on a zero-tolerance approach to drug use?
2. According to the author, what kind of legal discriminations do drug-war felons face upon release?
3. What are Nadelmann's concerns when drug counselors work with the criminal justice system?

Ethan Nadelmann, "Eroding Hopes for a Kinder, Gentler Drug Policy," *Drug Reporter*, www.alternet.org, July 29, 2002. Copyright © 2002 by AlterNet.org. Reproduced by permission.

The prevailing approach [to deal with drug use and abuse] in the United States is the war on drugs, which essentially is based on two presumptions: that the criminal justice system and other punitive mechanisms must play a central role in U.S. drug policy, and that the only permissible approach to drug use itself is zero tolerance. Drug policies are evaluated principally in terms of increases or decreases in the numbers of citizens who admit to using drugs illegally; the ultimate aim is a "drug-free" society.

The contending approach—advocated by the Drug Policy Alliance, the nation's leading drug policy reform organization, and by a growing drug policy reform movement in this country and abroad—is harm reduction. We believe that criminal justice measures to control drug use are mostly ineffective, counterproductive and unethical, and should generally be used as last, not first, resorts. We regard abstinence as a desirable way to avoid drug problems, but also insist that responsible users of psychoactive drugs should not be punished. We see the fantasy of a drug free society as foolish and potentially dangerous in its absolutism. Our ideal drug policy is one that most effectively reduces the death, disease, crime and suffering associated with both drug use and our largely failed drug control policies. And we insist on the need for fallback strategies, such as needle exchange or measures to stem fatal overdoses, to reduce the harms of drug use by and among those who cannot or will not stop using drugs today.

I have long assumed that drug abuse counselors—because they deal with drug abusers as human beings, and because so many once struggled with addiction themselves—must naturally be drawn to drug policy reform. But I also know that the trauma of drug addiction can distort clear analysis, that the constant search for government funding can compromise one's principles, and that relying on the criminal justice system to force people into treatment can prove highly seductive in dealing with people who can't or won't stop using drugs.

I listen to the Bush administration's statements and the response among many leaders in the treatment field, and fear that people who should know better are being co-opted by hollow rhetoric and a few more dollars thrown their direction.

There was much applause among treatment professionals when the administration announced its new drug control budget because it included $224 million (6.2%) more for drug treatment than the previous year. It seemed almost impolite to note that expenditures on prevention and research had dropped by $75 million (3%), spending on interdiction had increased by $215 million (10.4%), and that the basic ratio of federal expenditures on drug control remained essentially the same; twice as much for law enforcement and interdiction as for treatment and education. Behind the self-congratulation, the punitive priorities remain unchanged.

Federal Prisoners, by Offense—2002

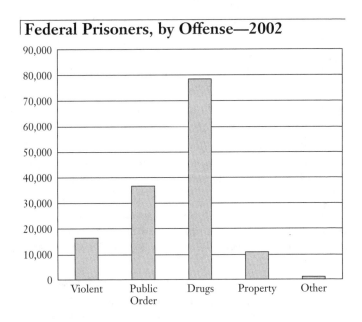

Bureau of Justice Statistics, 2002.

It's not enough, however, to focus just on the dollars allocated for drug treatment. Even more important are the policies that determine how these dollars are spent and how drug users, past and present, are treated. Drug treatment in the United States is mostly trapped inside an ideologically confined box that ill serves millions of people struggling with drug addiction. It's time to recognize the need for genuine diversity in addressing the infinite number of variables that determine why some people get in trouble with drugs and others do not. No single treatment approach—no matter how successful for some—can work for all.

Methadone maintenance, for example, remains stigmatized and ostracized in many parts of the country, a victim of misguided abstinence-only ideologies that disparage medical evidence. While Europe, Australia, Canada and other nations make this treatment available in pharmacies and doctors' offices and public health clinics, in the United States all but a few patients can obtain their medication only in heavily regulated clinics that may be far from their homes, poorly run, and staffed by personnel who are often hostile to methadone treatment. The former drug czar, Barry McCaffrey, at least gave lip service to making this treatment more readily available to those in need. The current drug czar so far has been silent.

If the planned expansion of buprenorphine maintenance ultimately leads to a diversification of oploid maintenance prescribing options—so that addiction treatment begins to resemble good pain management—then buprenorphine will have performed an important service. If buprenorphine instead provides an excuse for curtailing access to methadone and other maintenance options such as are now proliferating outside this country, it will result in more harm than good.

Legal Discriminations Impede Recovery

Perhaps the greatest contradiction in U.S. drug policy is that between the official rhetoric of helping people with drug problems and those in recovery, and the litany of legal discriminations that exacerbate drug problems and impede recovery. More than ten million Americans—maybe double that—have been convicted of drug offenses ranging from marijuana possession to sale of one illicit drug or another. The 1996 welfare reform act revokes welfare benefits for anyone convicted of a felony drug offense—for life. Under federal law, innocent family members of people who have used drugs can be evicted from public housing—even if the family members do not even know about the drug use. Otherwise law-abiding students are targeted as well: The federal Higher Education Act delays or denies eligibility for federal financial aid to any student convicted of any drug offense, no matter how minor. And in the wake of [the September 11, 2001, terrorist attacks], as private companies step up their background checks of current and potential employees, more and more people with minor drug offenses in their (often distant) past are finding themselves without a job.

None of these policies is consistent with good drug treatment—yet this administration, like its predecessor, has done nothing to repeal them; indeed, the perpetual search seems to focus on new and more onerous penalties. The single greatest challenge facing addiction counselors today concerns their relationship to the criminal justice system, and particularly to drug courts. The alternatives-to-incarceration movement has made important strides in diverting many drug offenders from courts and jails to treatment programs.

California's Proposition 36, for one, achieves this diversion while seeking to minimize the corruptions inherent in authorizing court supervision of an individual's drug treatment program. . . . State legislatures around the country are debating similar sorts of bills—all of which seek to improve and expand drug treatment options while reducing the use of incarceration in dealing with drug use and addiction.

But the popularity of drug courts and the increasing entanglement of criminal justice with treatment can come at a high price—the sacrifice of confidentiality between patient and caregiver; the diversion of government funding from voluntary and community-based treatment into coerced treatment programs, often behind bars; the propagation of a myth that treatment doesn't work unless it's backed by the state's coercive powers; the de facto criminalization of relapse; the need to treat non-problematic marijuana use as a basis for revocation of probation or parole; and so on.

State Coerced Abstinence

I fear that much of the treatment community has developed its own co-dependence—on the criminal justice system. That's where the money is, that's where the "market" is, and that's where one can turn when treatment "fails." Some drug court judges, I believe, are doing the Lord's work, but the institutionalization of the drug court model—where judges obsessed with dirty urines substitute their judgments for those of treatment professionals—may well corrupt drug treatment to the point that it becomes little more than a synonym for state-coerced abstinence.

The federal government's support for drug treatment does not extend far beyond its coercive aspects. Read closely the testimony of drug czar [John P.] Walters and DEA chief [Asa] Hutchinson. Listen to their speeches. And most especially watch their actions. This administration's bottom line on drug policy ultimately has little to do with helping people who struggle with drugs, much less those who have been arrested for a drug offense. Like the temperance warriors who shaped alcohol policy during the first decades of this century, their policies are really about punishing people for the sin of drug use.

Addiction counselors ultimately have to decide how much, and on what conditions they are willing to ally with and subordinate themselves to the criminal justice system in dealing with their clientele. This is an issue that goes to the heart of the profession. I only hope that this debate has begun in earnest, for it concerns the core values, the soul and the future of addiction counseling in America.

"Eliminating mandatory minimums for the least dangerous offenders is helping to free up space in overcrowded prisons to ensure that violent criminals remain locked up."

Mandatory Minimum Sentences Should Be Repealed

Part I: *USA Today;* Part II: Ron Walters

Federal mandatory minimum sentencing laws, enacted by Congress in 1986, require judges to deliver fixed sentences to individuals convicted of certain crimes, regardless of mitigating factors. According to the editors at *USA Today* in the following two-part viewpoint, repealing mandatory minimums for the least-dangerous offenders will help ensure that prisons have room for the most violent criminals, thus increasing public safety. *USA Today* is a nationwide daily newspaper also available in sixty countries worldwide. Ron Walters, a professor of government and politics at the University of Maryland at College Park, and director of the African American Leadership Institute, argues in his viewpoint that mandatory minimum sentencing has led to the lockup of an entire generation of black youths, who are targeted and punished at a greater rate than whites.

As you read, consider the following questions:

1. What are some suggested alternatives to replace mandatory minimum prison sentences as related by *USA Today?*
2. In Ron Walters's viewpoint, what group is working to confront and repeal mandatory minimum sentencing laws?

I

When a crime wave swept over American cities in the 1980s, states reacted with get-tough sentencing policies designed to take criminals off the street. From "three-time loser" laws that put away repeat offenders for life to long prison terms for drug convictions, states wanted to send a clear message: If you do the crime, you'll do the time.

Now tough economic times are prompting states to rethink that costly lockup strategy. [In 2003], the Delaware legislature approved reduced prison terms for some nonviolent drug offenders. In March, a repeal of Michigan's tough minimums went into effect, giving judges more discretion to set prison terms. And most other states are considering reforms of their sentencing laws.

The need by cash-strapped legislatures to close budget gaps may be the wrong reason to ease sentencing rules, but it is driving them to do the right thing. Eliminating mandatory minimums for the least-dangerous offenders is helping to free up space in overcrowded prisons to ensure that violent criminals remain locked up.

That would be good news if the releases were thought out carefully to solve the problems of inflexible mandatory sentencing rules. Trouble is, some states have let their budget woes drive their prison policies. The result: equally rigid rules that decide which criminals get back on the street.

In Kentucky, for example, the state last year [2002] ordered every prisoner convicted of non-violent drug and property crimes to be released 90 days early. That plan was suspended this year [2003] after an outcry over repeat offenses committed by some new parolees.

Other states, by contrast, have adopted more sensible sentencing reforms that have helped them cut their budgets without increasing their crime rates. Some examples:

• Michigan. It eliminated minimum sentences, including lifetime parole for minor drug possession. The move is expected to save $41 million a year and lead to the release of more than 1,100 inmates, some sentenced to 200 years for non-violent offenses.

• Washington. A law that went into effect this year reduces sentences for minor drug offenses, saving $8 million annually in prison costs. The state is funneling some of that money into drug-treatment programs.

Defenders of mandatory minimums say those stiff sentences reduce crime. They point to a falling crime rate in the past decade, including a drop in murders from 9.6 per 100,000 people in 1991 to 5.6 in 2002.

Long sentences do deter crime—when they keep dangerous criminals off the street. Yet Northeastern University criminologist James Fox says that goal is undercut when those who commit violent crimes not covered by mandatory sentences receive short terms to make room for all of the non-violent drug offenders filling U.S. prisons.

One-fourth of prisoners are drug offenders, and the overwhelming majority have not committed violent crimes, according to the Justice Department. While handing them 50- to 200-year sentences helps politicians look as if they are tough on crime, those stiff terms don't actually reduce crime, according to studies by liberal, conservative and nonpartisan groups.

That's why mindless sentencing policies need to be corrected—as long as the answer isn't mindless release plans.

II

I was watching a hearing of the House of Representatives Subcommittee on Appropriations on the needs of the Supreme Court. It was chaired by Virginia Rep. Frank Wolf and featured Justices Anthony Kennedy and Clarence Thomas. I was noting that there seemed to be a division of labor between the two justices. Thomas apparently was sent there to testify about the administrative and technological needs of the high court, while Kennedy explained staffing needs and other issues.

They were talking about their respective issues when Wolf asked Kennedy about his pursuit of eliminating mandatory minimums. I was startled at the passion with which Kennedy responded, stating that the United States now incarcerates people at eight times more than any industrial country in the world and that 55 percent of those in the federal system are there for petty drug offenses.

Increase in State and Federal Prison Commitments, 1978–1996

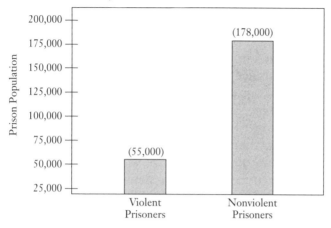

"America's One Million Nonviolent Prisoners," Center on Juvenile and Criminal Justice, March 1999.

Kennedy plowed on, saying that such sentences were "unfair, unjust, and unwise . . ." and that the guidelines were put into place at a time when politicians were trying to outdo one another in being "tough on crime." The goal was to give everybody the same sentence. Since it was thought that no one actually served the sentences meted out by the courts, long sentences, it was concluded, would be deterrents.

Kennedy also suggested that the sentencing has been too expensive. California was spending $26,000 on inmates locked up for this purpose and just $6,000 on education per child at the level of elementary education.

Wolf struck back, saying that we are becoming a violent society and that he would be for possibly adjusting the sentences for nonviolent offenders, but not for violent ones. For example, he talked about taking the money used to incarcerate offenders and putting it into drug-rehabilitation programs. If people violated their drug-rehabilitation program, then they would do time—or some other such formulation.

Kennedy shot back with the thought that supervised release has been found to be 40 percent more effective and cheaper than having someone in full-time custody, and that since the court system has to spend more money to allocate resources for mandatory minimums, we are not doing a good job. Kennedy ended his passionate charge to the conservative lawmakers in front him by praising the courage of justices who served lower level courts that were not following the minimum guidelines.

A group called Families Against Mandatory Minimum Sentences has grown up to confront and repeal this pernicious law. The Hip-Hop mogul Russell Simons has been waging a campaign in New York City to bring heat and light to the opposition to this issue. But I have not seen the rest of our leadership out front on this issue that, more than any other, has contributed to locking up an entire generation of Black youth who are targeted and punished at a greater rate than Whites.

These young people have been caught up in a nasty period of ideological fervor, in which White males had to prove that they in fact controlled society by fashioning a set of laws into the 1994 Omnibus Crime Bill. This bill has had a disastrous effect on our community, even at a time when crime has been going down. So, even though 6,000 of them will be coming out this year, most will not be eligible for public housing, student loans, and other public goods that will enable them to get a fresh start in society.

President [George W.] Bush adopted a program created by Jesse Jackson that proposed to put churches in a relationship to those coming out of prison, to make their transition easier. But nothing would make it easier than to eliminate those punishment laws that have made it tough for them to get a new start and easier for them to consider giving up and going back to their old ways. In fact, Bush ought to make it harder for them to get in, rather than easier to get out, but he's made it impossible to get on with their lives.

The Black leadership has said a lot about getting convicted felons to vote, but not much about getting them a life, and we are giving the politicians a pass on this issue. For example, if you go to [presidential candidate in 2004] John Kerry's Web site, there is a list of issues, but nothing about the repeal of mandatory minimums—or any other criminal-justice issue. Democrats have also played the game of being "tough on crime" to stay viable in the race for votes. But it is time to know where Kerry stands (we know where Bush stands) on this issue.

Justice Clarence Thomas said not a mumbling word at the hearing, but Kennedy and his colleague Justice Steven Breyer are fighting hard. We should join them.

Periodical Bibliography

The following articles have been selected to supplement the diverse views presented in this chapter.

Jodi L. Avergun "Defending America's Most Vulnerable: Safe Access to Drug Treatment and Child Protection Act of 2005—H.R. 1528," Statement Before the House Judiciary Committee Subcommittee on Crime, Terrorism and Homeland Security, April 12, 2005. www.judiciary.house.gov.

Chauncey Bailey "Black Legislators: Drug War Has Failed," *Sun Reporter*, Jan 2, 2005.

Radley Balko "The Drug War Toll Mounts," Cato Institute, December 2, 2004. www.cato.org.

Bruce L. Benson and David W. Rasmussen "Illicit Drugs and Crime," *Independent Institute Policy Report*, 2005. www.independent.org.

Rick Brand "What Is Just and Fair?" *Daily Dispatch*, June 8, 2005. ww.hendersondispatch.com.

Kathy Dix "Criminal Element: Silent Infectious Invaders from the U.S. Correctional System," *Infection Control Today*, July 27, 2005. www.infection controltoday.com.

Ruth Wilson Gilmore "Spend Cash on Schools, Not on Building Prisons," *Los Angeles Daily News*, June 30, 2005.

Alberto Gonzales "Sentencing Guidelines Speech," National Center for Victims of Crime First National Conference, Washington, DC, June 21, 2005. www.usdoj.gov.

Carolyn Hileman "Prison Scandal," *Land of the Free*, July 19, 2005. www.thelandofthefree.net.

Laura Jones "Unjust Mandatory Minimums Strike Again: Weldon Angelos Sentenced to 55 Years and 1 Day in Prison," *Sentencing News*, November 16, 2004. www.famm.org

Lenora Lapidus et al. "Caught in the Net: The Impact of Drug Policies on Women and Their Families," American Civil Liberties Union, March 22, 2005. www.aclu.org.

Eli Lehrer "Crime Without Punishment: As American Streets Get Safer, Crime in Europe Soars," *Weekly Standard*, May 27, 2002. www.weekly standard.com.

Barbara Levine	"Local Comment: Less Prisons, More Parolees," *Detroit Free Press*, July 5, 2005.
Adrian Levy and Cathy Scott-Clark	"Afghanistan: 'One Huge US Jail,'" *Guardian/ UK*, March 19, 2005.
Iain Murray	"Incapacitate Yes, Rehabilitate No," *American Enterprise*, April/May 2005.
Chuck Poochigian	"Let's Keep California Tough on Crime," *Tracy Press*, February 9, 2005. www.republican.sen. ca.gov.
Dan Seligman	"Lock 'Em Up," *Forbes*, May 23, 2005.

CHAPTER 2

Are Prisons Just?

Chapter Preface

Reports of human rights abuses by American military, CIA personnel, and civilian interrogators of Iraqi prisoners at Abu Ghraib prison in 2004 ignited a firestorm of criticism against American military personnel and procedures. Newspapers across the world printed photographs showing nude and bound Iraqi prisons being humiliated by U.S. soldiers. An unexpected twist came when allegations surfaced that such abuses had long been common at U.S. domestic prisons. Robert Perkinson, assistant professor of American studies at the University of Hawaii, reported that Specialist Charles Graner, identified as a ringleader in the Abu Ghraib prison abuses, had worked at a Pennsylvania supermaximum security prison notorious for "racist guards, routine beatings and elaborate rituals of humiliation." Deborah Davies, in her BBC investigative report "Torture in America's Brutal Prisons" claimed that "Abu Ghraib, far from being the work of a few rogue individuals, was simply the export of the worst practices that take place in the domestic prison system all the time."

Not unexpectedly, many prison officials and law enforcement personnel hotly denied these charges. The Bureau of Prisons pointed out that convicted criminals are sent to prison *as* punishment, not *for* punishment, and that "administrative remedies exist for addressing allegations of abuse." Skeptics asserted that prison opponents trumped up human rights abuse charges to discredit America's prisons system generally. According to these analysts, the charges had no basis in fact.

In the following chapter various authors present their views on whether or not U.S. prisons are just. The question is a critical one. As Nicholas Katzenback, cochair of the Commission on Safety and Abuse in America's Prisons, contends, "What happens in prison and jail affects the very fabric of our society." Just as the Abu Ghraib prison scandal tarnished the reputation of the military in the eyes of many, so too have charges of abuse at America's domestic prisons led many Americans to wonder if U.S. prisons are just.

"*We manage our institutions through meaningful communication and constructive interaction between staff and inmates.*"

U.S. Prisons Are Humane

Harley G. Lappin

Harley G. Lappin is the director of the federal Bureau of Prisons. In this viewpoint Lappin describes to members of the U.S. House of Representatives the programs and operations of the federal Bureau of Prisons. Lappin contends that the bureau maintains safe, humane, and cost-efficient facilities despite a nearly seven-fold increase in the federal prison population and system-wide crowding. The bureau provides educational and drug abuse treatment programs that Lappin considers essential to effective inmate management and vital to helping inmates adopt a crime-free lifestyle upon release.

As you read, consider the following questions:

1. What factors does Lappin cite as contributing to prison overcrowding?
2. Which inmates are subject to regular urinalysis, according to the author? Why?
3. As reported by Lappin, to what types of jobs are most federal prisoners assigned?

Harley G. Lappin, statement before the U.S. House Subcommittee on Crime, Committee on the Judiciary, Washington, DC, May 14, 2003.

The [Bureau of Prisons] continues to effectively meet our mission to protect society by confining offenders in facilities that are safe, humane, cost-efficient, and appropriately secure, and that provide work and other self-improvement opportunities to assist offenders in becoming law-abiding citizens. Earlier this year [2003], we added to our strategic plan a new goal, to enhance our efforts regarding the prevention, disruption, and response to terrorist activities.

The Federal inmate population has increased nearly sevenfold in the last two decades, from approximately 25,000 inmates and 41 institutions in 1980 to more than 169,000 inmates and 103 institutions [in 2003]. . . .

To address this population growth, the Bureau's budget has grown from approximately $330 million in 1980 to more than $4.4 billion. . . .

Facilities and Crowding

The Bureau confines inmates in institutions at four security levels (minimum, low, medium, and high) and has one maximum-security prison for the less than 1 percent of Bureau of Prisons inmates who require that level of security. The Bureau also operates detention centers (that confine mostly pretrial detainees and presentenced offenders) and Federal medical centers that provide medical care to inmates who cannot be housed in general population facilities.

The rapid growth of the inmate population has led to system-wide crowding of 37 percent above the rated capacity, with the most severe crowding at medium-security and high-security institutions (which are 60 and 53 percent above capacity, respectively). These crowding rates, however, will decrease with the activation of 7 new facilities in 2004, 4 medium-security and 3 high-security prisons ($252 million). Prison crowding contributes to increased inmate idleness due to an increased demand on programs and services. With the support of Congress, the Bureau is making every effort to ensure that sufficient staff are available in its facilities to provide adequate prisoner supervision and to offset the deleterious effects of crowding on inmate management. . . .

We manage our institutions through meaningful communication and constructive interaction between staff and inmates. The Bureau believes that this approach ensures accountability, allows us to gather intelligence, encourages positive inmate behavior, and helps the Bureau address inmates' concerns before they become serious problems. In addition, regardless of the specific discipline in which a staff member works, all employees are "correctional workers first." This means that everyone, from secretaries to correctional officers to wardens, is responsible for the security and good order of the institution. All staff are expected to be vigilant and attentive to inmate accountability and security issues, to respond to emergencies, and to maintain a proficiency in security matters, as well as in their particular job specialty. In addition, all Bureau institutions have a comprehensive employee development program, including formal training programs, and mentoring by experienced staff.

Safety and Security

The Bureau of Prisons employs a validated inmate classification system to designate inmates to correctional facilities that provide the appropriate level of security and supervision. This system minimizes the likelihood that vulnerable offenders will be confined with predators or that first time non-violent offenders will be confined with sophisticated and dangerous criminals.

In recent years, the Bureau has improved prison design and construction, made many physical plant improvements, and taken advantage of technological developments to further enhance institution security, including the use of closed-circuit video recording equipment to detect and deter illicit inmate activities. In order to control illegal drug use in Federal prisons, institution staff routinely search inmates and their property. In addition, the Bureau regularly conducts urinalysis on random samples of inmates as well as members of disruptive groups, inmates who are suspected of using. . . drugs, and inmates who have an institutional history of the possession, use, or distribution of drugs. Inmates are subject to disciplinary action if they test positive for a controlled substance or if they refuse to provide a urine sample. The Bureau has experienced significant reductions in assaults (on both staff and other inmates), homicides, suicides, escapes from secure institutions and other serious misconduct over the past several years.

Inmate Care and Programming

The Bureau helps protect society from criminal activity by encouraging inmates to participate in a range of programs that will help them adopt a crime-free lifestyle upon their return to the community. These programs are an essential component of effective inmate management, and they are as important to the security and good order of Federal prisons as fences, daily counts, and searches.

All sentenced inmates in Federal correctional institutions are required to work, except for the relatively small number who for security, educational, or medical reasons are unable to do so. Most inmates are assigned to institutional maintenance jobs such as a food service worker, orderly, plumber, painter, warehouse worker, or groundskeeper. Due to current levels of crowding, most work details are comprised of more inmates than necessary to accomplish the particular task. Staff must be continually creative to provide sufficient work opportunities. Approximately 22 percent of the Bureau's medically able, sentenced inmates work in Federal Prison Industries (FPI), the Bureau's most important correctional program. . . .

FPI directly contributes to public safety by providing inmates with skills necessary to successfully reintegrate into society after release from prison.

Rigorous research has demonstrated that inmates who worked in prison industries were 24 percent less likely to recidivate than those who did not, and were 14 percent more likely to be employed following release from prison than their non-participating peers. . . .

In Fiscal Year 2002, inmates working in FPI paid $3 million for victim restitution, fines, and child support.

The Bureau is getting significantly greater numbers of Federal inmates who are serving more time in prison, are unskilled, undereducated, criminally sophisticated, and physically violent. Virtually all of these inmates will be released back into our neighborhoods at some point and will need work skills if they are to successfully reintegrate into society.

FPI creates the opportunity for inmates to work in diversified work programs that teach work skills and a work ethic, both of which can lead to viable employment upon release. . . .

Medical Care

Inmates typically have greater health care needs than the average citizen. Many offenders have long-standing medical, dental, and psychiatric concerns which either have been neglected in the past, or which have resulted from dysfunctional lifestyles involving drugs or alcohol abuse. The Bureau has developed and implemented several major health services initiatives designed to enhance efficiency and effectiveness of the Bureau's medical care. These include an increased emphasis on managed care and the management of infectious diseases. . . .

In addition to substantial medical needs, many inmates are in need of some form of mental health care. Psychologists at Bureau of Prisons facilities offer inmates a range of psychological services and programs that include: initial psychological assessment, crisis intervention, suicide prevention, counseling, individual psychotherapy, and group psychotherapy. Additionally, psychologists offer inmates a number of specialty treatment programs to assist them in gaining greater insight into their specific psychological disorder(s) and in developing the skills needed to successfully overcome their problem(s).

Education and Drug Abuse Programs

All Bureau of Prisons institutions offer a variety of education programs and occupational and vocational training programs based on the vocational training needs of the inmates, general labor market conditions, and institution labor force needs. Through all of these programs, inmates gain knowledge and skills that help them become gainfully employed upon release and avoid new criminal conduct. These programs have been shown to significantly reduce recidivism, and the Bureau is committed to addressing the education deficits with which inmates begin their incarceration. At present, just over one-third of all inmates are enrolled in one or more educational classes.

The Prison Population Keeps Climbing

Some 2.21 million persons—or one in every 140 U.S. residents—were incarcerated at year end 2003, according to statistics in Prisoners in 2003, a bulletin of the Bureau of Justice Statistics. . . .

Among [the bulletin's] highlights:

• The nation's largest system, the Federal Bureau of Prisons, grew 5.8 percent—the same as in 2002.

• State prison population grew by 1.6 percent, less than the 2.4 percent growth in 2002.

• Prison population increased by five percent in 11 states, led by North Dakota (up 11.4 percent), Minnesota (up 10.3 percent) and Montana (up 8.9 percent).

• Eleven states had prison population decreases, led by Connecticut (down 4.2 percent), New York (down 2.8 percent), Michigan (down 2.4 percent), and New Jersey (down 2.3 percent).

• Privately operated facilities housed 95,522 prisoners (5.7 percent of state and 12.6 percent of federal prisoners). Since the end of 2000, the number of federal prisoners in private facilities increased more than 40 percent, but the number of state prisoners in private facilities declined 1.8 percent.

• Federal prisons were operating at 39 percent above capacity; state prisons were estimated to be at capacity to 16 percent above capacity.

• Race and ethnicity of federal and state prisoners changed little since 1995: 44 percent black, 35 percent white, 19 percent Hispanic and 2 percent other races.

• In 2003 an estimated 388,700 sentenced state and federal inmates were between the ages of 40 and 54—up from 236,000 in 1995—and accounted for about 46 percent of growth in the sentenced population since 1995.

FAMM GRAM, Winter 2004.

The Bureau requires that, with few exceptions, inmates who do not have a verified 12th-grade education participate in the literacy program for a minimum of 240 hours or until they obtain the GED credential. Non-English speaking inmates are required to participate in an English as a Second Language program until they are proficient in oral and written English. Institutions also offer literacy classes and adult continuing education. . . .

The cornerstone of the Bureau's drug abuse treatment programming is the residential drug abuse treatment program which is provided in 50 Bureau institutions. The treatment is designed for inmates with moderate to serious substance abuse disorders, about 34 percent of the Bureau's population. The residential drug abuse program is a course of individual and group treatment, lasting 9 months in residential treatment units set apart from the general prison population. Treatment is provided 3 to 4 hours a day, 5 days a week, and follows a cognitive behavioral treatment model. When not on the treatment unit, the inmate spends his or her time in educational programs, work, vocational training, or other inmate programs that are available at the institution. Upon completion of the residential drug abuse treatment program, the inmate must continue his or her treatment in the general population and/or in a community corrections center. This follow-up treatment is essential in preventing and detecting relapse, thereby enhancing community safety. . . .

Encouraged by the positive results of the residential substance abuse treatment program, the Bureau has implemented a number of new residential programs for special populations (including younger, high security, and intractable, quick-tempered inmates) who are responsible for much of the misconduct that occurs in Federal prisons. The cognitive restructuring approach used in the drug treatment programs was carried over as the foundation for programs to change the criminal thinking and behavior patterns of inmates. These programs focus on inmates' emotional and behavioral responses to difficult situations. While too early to assess value in terms of reducing recidivism, we have found that these programs significantly reduce inmates' involvement in institution misconduct. In general, a strong relationship exists between institution misconduct and recidivism, so we are hopeful that the full evaluations of these programs will confirm their effect in reducing recidivism. . . .

Religious Programs

The Bureau of Prisons' religious programs are intended to provide inmates with opportunities to grow spiritually and to strengthen their religious convictions. Bureau institutions schedule services and meeting times for inmates of the approximately 30 faiths represented within the population. Religious programs are led or supervised by staff chaplains, contract spiritual leaders, and community volunteers of a variety of faiths. Chaplains provide and oversee inmate worship services and self-improvement forums such as scripture study and religious workshops and are available upon request to provide pastoral care, spiritual guidance, and counseling to inmates. Inmates may also request spiritual counseling from community representatives. Inmates are able to observe religious holy days and are able to wear and use religious items consistent with both their faith and with the security, safety, and good order of the institution. An alternative diet is available to those inmates whose religious beliefs include special diets.

The Bureau has developed a residential faith-based pre-release pilot program for male and female inmates of various security levels. The pilot sites are FMC Carswell, Texas; FCI Milan, Michigan; FCI Petersburg, Virginia; FCI Victorville, California; and USP Leavenworth, Kansas. The program—which is voluntary and open to inmates of any faith—aims to reduce crime and recidivism by providing participants with moral and spiritual principles that can influence their future decisions. There is a growing body of empirical evidence that demonstrates the potency of faith in changing behavior. This model initiative has a strong mentoring component during the pre-release phase and post-prison aftercare component designed to offer moral guidance and a caring community to help ex-offenders reenter society with hope and responsibility.

All of the Bureau's inmate programs are intended to prepare inmates for a successful return to the community. In fact, immediately upon their admission to Federal prison, offenders are encouraged to begin planning for their eventual release and to start to assume a productive and successful lifestyle. The Bureau complements its array of programs with a specific Release Preparation Program in which inmates become involved near the end of their sentence.

"Squalor and harsh treatment are the intended result of the get-tough, no-frills penal values expressed by some of our country's most powerful policymakers."

U.S. Prisons Are Not Humane

Judith Greene

Judith Greene is a criminal justice policy analyst and a research associate with Families Against Mandatory Minimums and the Justice Policy Institute. In the following viewpoint Greene examines what she terms the "harsh prison culture" in the United States. According to Greene, access to job training, education, and substance abuse treatment in prison has diminished. In U.S. prisons, Greene reports, women, men, and even youth are subjected to violent and demeaning abuse, and control of prisoners is maintained through high-tech surveillance systems, immobilizing restraints, pepper spray, stun devices, and isolation cells. She asserts that prison reform will require a fundamental shift in attitudes and values among the American people, who largely support the idea that prison should be harsh and punitive.

As you read consider the following questions:
1. In Greene's view, what circumstances have led to America's harsh prison culture?
2. What effect does the Prison Litigation Reform Act have on prisoners seeking relief, according to the author?
3. What steps does Greene propose to improve conditions in U.S. prisons?

Judith Greene, "Examining Our Harsh Prison Culture," *Ideas for an Open Society*, vol. 4, October 2004. Copyright © 2004 by the Open Society Institute. Reproduced by permission.

To a great extent, the rapid increase in incarceration over the past quarter century and a shift in the demographic makeup of the U.S. prison population have given rise to our country's harsh prison culture. Tough-on-crime policies and draconian sentencing laws have expanded the prison population at unaffordable and unmanageable rates. And the War on Drugs has not only increased the size of our prison population but also heavily skewed the population mix toward people of color.

At the same time, as crime policies hardened, attitudes about the treatment of people in prison coarsened. Prison policy moved away from the basic principles that correctional services must be effective, accountable, and humane. Spurred by the cynical use of get-tough rhetoric by public officials seeking political gain, a popular mentality developed that celebrates the notion that prisoners deserve sadistic and brutal treatment as punishment. Against this backdrop, massive prison expansion has occurred, entailing the construction of bigger facilities, in remote locations, with few amenities or services. Diminished opportunities for education, vocational training, and substance abuse treatment mean more idle time, which leads to increased tension and violence among prisoners.

Such prisons present difficult management challenges. Unfortunately, the response has been to increase reliance on high-tech surveillance systems, immobilizing restraints, and weaponry including chemical agents and pepper spray, stun devices, and (in a few prison systems) armed guards with orders to shoot if disturbances arise. Total isolation of those deemed dangerous has become so widespread that entire prisons have been constructed for this purpose. These supermax facilities provide the ultimate means for warehousing people—many are held for months or years in solitary confinement cells, often denied even reading material to pass the time. Such psychosis-inducing regimes generate the very behaviors that they are designed to curb.

Squalid and Brutal

Of the more than 2 million people confined in our prisons and jails, many are well acquainted with humiliating strip searches, inadequate and sometimes rotten food, and the denial of medical care, medications, and mental health treatment. Videotapes have documented the excessive force used by guards in Arkansas, California, Connecticut, Pennsylvania, and Texas. And lawsuits have exposed the sexual abuse of incarcerated women by guards in Connecticut, Georgia, Michigan, and New Jersey.

In Virginia's Wallens Ridge supermax facility, prisoners have been immobilized in five-point restraints for as long as 48 hours. After a man died following repeated shocks from an Ultron II stun device, the American Civil Liberties Union filed a class-action lawsuit charging that the use of excessive force was endemic in the prison.

A privately operated prison for youths in Jena, Louisiana was closed in 2000 after experts sent by the U.S. Department of Justice to inspect the facility reported that the environment was neither safe nor humane, and that operations were chaotic and dangerous. Medical, mental health, and dental services were inadequate to meet the needs of the 276 young men confined there; education and substance abuse programs were deficient: clothing and linens were insufficient; and the staff used both chemical agents and physical restraints improperly and subjected the prisoners to physical, sexual, and verbal abuse.

After years of pressure by youth advocates, a second prison—this one operated by the Louisiana Department of Public Safety and Corrections—was shuttered on June 1, 2004. In her searing exposé, "The Death of Tallulah Prison," Soros Justice Fellow Xochitl Bervera charged that conditions at the prison in Tallulah were hardly better than in Jena, and that conditions are "startlingly violent and demeaning" throughout the entire youth prison system in Louisiana: "Children routinely face humiliation and other forms of emotional abuse as well as severe physical abuse at the hands of guards. . . . Only nine months ago, 17-year-old Emmanuelle Narcisse was killed by a guard in another of Louisiana's facilities by a single blow to the head that was witnessed by dozens of other children."

Why are our prisons such miserable places? Notwithstanding the huge expenditure of state and federal dollars on the construction of high-tech facilities, America's jails and prisons remain mostly squalid, brutal institutions. And all the more so, since squalor and harsh treatment are the intended result of the get-tough, no-frills penal values expressed by some of our country's most powerful policymakers.

Scars, Pain, and Death

In American prisons today, wanton staff brutality and degrading treatment of inmates occurs across the country with distressing frequency. . . .

In recent years, U.S. prison inmates have been beaten with fists and batons, stomped on, kicked, shot, stunned with electronic devices, doused with chemical sprays, choked, and slammed face first onto concrete floors by the officers whose job it is to guard them. Inmates have ended up with broken jaws, smashed ribs, perforated eardrums, missing teeth, burn scars—not to mention psychological scars and emotional pain. Some have died. . . .

Even detained children and youth are not immune from staff brutality and abuse.

Jamie Fellner, "Prisoner Abuse: How Different Are U.S. Prisons?" June 7, 2004. www.november.org.

Arizona Sheriff Joe Arpaio is revered and emulated for his tough-talking, retributive regime: holding people in tents in blistering desert heat and forcing them to wear pink underpants, eat green baloney sandwiches, and labor on "equal opportunity" chain gangs for men, women, and children. Where degradation and humiliation are a matter of policy, racial tensions go unchecked, and guards hold near-absolute authority, abuse and brutality inevitably follow.

Exporting Cruelty

While some have speculated that the reports of harsh treatment from prisons and detention camps in Iraq indicate the existence of policy at a high level of government, experienced observers of conditions in U.S. prisons are quick to recognize that the Abu Ghraib photos [which showed American soldiers abusing Iraqi prisoners] reek of the cruel but usual methods of control used by many U.S. prison personnel. Our vengeful penal philosophy and harsh prison culture has led to a dreadful level of brutality and human rights abuses in our own prisons, and now this maliciously punitive mentality has been exported to Iraq by U.S. prison personnel.

The Abu Ghraib prison was restored to operation by Lane McCotter, a U.S. prison consultant handpicked by the U.S. Department of Justice for the job. In 1997, McCotter had resigned as the director of the Utah Department of Corrections amid controversy following the death of a mentally ill man who had been strapped in a restraint chair for 16 hours. McCotter was under fire already for his handling of problems with medical and mental healthcare when it came to light that the psychiatrist who authorized the restraint was on probation by state licensing authorities for a variety of fraudulent and questionable practices.

Tier 1A, where Iraqis were held for interrogation by army intelligence personnel, was largely staffed with inexperienced and untrained soldiers who said they turned for leadership to Staff Sergeant Ivan H. Frederick and Specialist Charles A. Graner. Under leadership from men who honed their skills as prison guards in the U.S., the raw recruits assigned to guard Tier 1A took degradation and humiliation to new heights. In the photos that they made, they appear delighted with their handiwork.

Restoring Human Dignity

Back in U.S. prisons, routine abuse and widespread violations of human rights remain largely below the public radar, and the Prison Litigation Reform Act (PLRA), enacted by Congress in 1996, has greatly restricted access for prisoners to legal redress of substandard conditions of confinement and mistreatment by guards. If the shocking exposure of prison abuses in Iraq draws attention to the need to change conditions in our prisons, a roll-back of PLRA restrictions would be a good place to start.

An effort to improve conditions in U.S. prisons would require better training of prison guards, stronger enforcement of standards by prison managers, and free and frequent access to all prisons for independent human rights monitors and the media. But because approval, even celebration, of Arpaio-style punishment is now so prevalent in our popular culture, a serious effort would require more than better prison management and public oversight. Prison reform would require a fundamental shift in attitudes and values: the firm rejection of humiliating and degrading practices intended to inflict suffering, and the realization that incarcerated people are human beings and as such are deserving of simple human dignity and respect. But what is needed most to diminish the misery that permeates the penal system is a thorough overhaul of the harsh sentencing laws and policies that have driven the prison system to this unmanageable scale.

*"Black incarceration rates reflect deep bias
in the criminal justice system."*

The Prison System Is Racist

Paul Street

America's prison system discriminates against African Americans, maintains Paul Street in the following viewpoint. He argues that African Americans are incarcerated at vastly higher rates than are whites. In addition, he points out, supervision in these prisons is largely by whites. According to Street, these racist practices have devastating political and economic effects on African American communities. Street is director of research at the Chicago Urban League. His articles have appeared in numerous publications, including *In These Times, Z Magazine, Monthly Review,* and *Journal of American Ethnic History.*

As you read, consider the following questions:
1. According to the author, what percentage of African Americans are "under correctional supervision" on any given day?
2. As argued by Street, why is the criminal justice system haunted by "echoes of slavery"?
3. What type of communities benefit from the prison construction boom, in the author's opinion?

Defined simply as overt public bigotry, racism in the United States has fallen to an all-time low. Understood in socioeconomic, political and institutional terms, however, American racism is as alive as ever. More than thirty years after the heroic victories of the civil rights movement, Stanley Aronowitz [a professor of sociology at the City University of New York] notes, "the stigma of race remains the unmeltable condition of the black social and economic situation." Consider a *Chicago Tribune* article that appeared well off the front page, under the title "Towns Put Dreams in Prisons." In downstate Hoopeston, Illinois, there is "talk of the mothballed canneries that once made this a boom town and whether any of that bustling spirit might return if the Illinois Department of Corrections comes to town." Seeking jobs and economic growth, Hoopeston's leaders are negotiating with state officials for the right to host a shiny new maximum-security correctional facility. "You don't like to think about incarceration," Hoopeston's Mayor is quoted as saying, "but this is an opportunity for Hoopeston. We've been plagued by plant closings." The mayor's judgment is seconded in the *Tribune*'s account of the considerable benefits, including dramatically increased tax revenues, that flowed to Ina, Illinois, after it signed up to become a prison town a few years ago.

Two things are missing from this story. The first is an appropriate sense of horror at the spectacle of a society in which local officials are reduced to lobbying for prisons as their best chance for economic growth. The second concerns the matter of race. Nowhere did the reporter or his informants (insofar as they are fully and accurately recorded) mention either the predominantly white composition of the keepers or the predominantly black composition of the kept in the prison towns that increasingly look to the mass incarceration boom as the solution to their economic problems. As everyone knows, but few like to discuss, the mostly white residents of those towns are building their economic "dreams" on the transport and lockdown of unfree African-Americans from impoverished inner-city neighborhoods in places like Chicago, Rockford, East St. Louis, and Rock Island.

The New Racism: America's Prison System

This second absence is consistent with the politically correct rules of the new racism that plagues the United States at the turn of the millennium. There is a widespread belief among whites—deeply and ironically reinforced by the demise of open public racial prejudice—that African-Americans now enjoy equal and color-blind opportunity. "As white America sees it," write Leonard Steinhorn and Barbara Diggs-Brown in their sobering "By the Color of Their Skin: The Illusion of Integration and the Reality of Race," "Every effort has been made to welcome blacks into the American mainstream, and now they're on their own. . . . 'We got the message, we made the corrections—get on with it.'" "Going Downstate" Corrections, indeed. Nowhere, perhaps, is the persistence and even resurgence of racism more evident than in America's burgeoning "correctional" system. At the start of the twenty-first century, blacks are 12.3 percent of U.S. population, but they make up fully half of the roughly two million Americans currently behind bars. On any given day, 30 percent of African-American males ages 20 to 29 are "under correctional supervision"—either in jail or prison or on probation or parole. And according to a chilling statistical model used by the Bureau of Justice Statistics, a young black man age sixteen in 1996 faces a 29 percent chance of spending time in prison during his life. The corresponding statistic for white men in the same age group is 4 percent. The remarkable number and percentage of persons locked up by the state or otherwise under the watchful eye of criminal justice authorities in the United States—far beyond those of the rest of the industrialized world—is black to an extraordinary degree.

This harsh reality gives rise to extreme racial dichotomies. Take, for example, the different meanings of the phrase "going downstate" for youths of different skin colors in the Chicago metropolitan area. For many white teens, those words evoke the image of a trip with Mom and Dad to begin academic careers at the prestigious University of Illinois at Urbana-Champaign or at one of the state's many other public universities. But for younger Chicago-area blacks, especially males (just 6 percent of the state's prisoners are female), "going downstate" more likely connotes a trip under armed guard to begin prison careers at one of the state's numerous maximum- or medium-security prisons. Indeed, Illinois has 149,525 more persons enrolled in its four-year public universities than in its prisons. When it comes to blacks, who make up 12.25 percent of the public university population, it has 5,500 more prisoners, making blacks 66 percent of the state's prisoners. For every African-American enrolled in those universities, at least two are in prison or on parole in Illinois.

Similar differences of meaning can be found in other states with significant black populations. In New York, where the relevant phrase is "going upstate," the Justice Policy Institute and the Correctional Association of New York report that in the 1990s more blacks entered prison just for drug offenses than graduated from the state's massive university system with undergraduate, masters, and doctoral degrees combined. In some inner-city neighborhoods, researchers and advocates report, a preponderant majority of black males now possess criminal records. Criminologists Dina Rose and Todd Clear have found black neighborhoods in Tallahassee, Florida, where every resident can identify at least one friend or relative who has been incarcerated. In many predominantly black urban communities across the country, it appears, incarceration is so widespread and commonplace that it has become what the U.S. Bureau of Justice Statistics director Jan Chaiken recently called "almost a normative life experience." Boys are growing up with the sense that it is standard for older brothers, uncles, fathers, cousins, and, perhaps, someday, themselves to be locked up by the state.

Labor Market Disenfranchisement

Researchers and advocates tracking the impact of mass incarceration find devastating consequences in high-poverty black communities. The most well known is the widespread political disenfranchisement of felons and ex-felons. The economic effects are equally significant. African-Americans are disproportionately and often deeply disenfranchised in competitive job markets by low skills, poor schools, weakened family structures, racial discrimination in hiring and promotion, and geographic isolation from the leading sectors of job growth. When prison and felony records are thrown into that mixture, the results can be disastrous. It is not uncommon to hear academic researchers and service providers cite unemployment rates as high as 50 percent for people with criminal records. One study, based in California during the early 1990s, found that just 21 percent of that state's parolees were working full time. In a detailed study, Karen Needels found that less than 40 percent of 1,176 men released from Georgia's prison system in 1976 had any officially recorded earnings in each year from 1983 to 1991. For those with earnings, average annual wages were exceedingly low and differed significantly by race: white former inmates averaged $7,880 per year and blacks made $4,762. In the most widely cited study in the growing literature on the labor market consequences of racially disparate criminal justice policies, Harvard economist Richard Freeman used data from the National Longitudinal Survey of Youth (NLSY). Limiting his sample to out-of-school men and controlling for numerous variables (drug usage, education, region, and age) that might bias upward the link between criminal records and weak labor market attachment, Freeman found that those who had been in jail or on probation in 1980 had a 19 percent higher chance of being unemployed in 1988 than those with no involvement in the criminal justice system. He also found that prison records reduced the amount of time employed after release by 25 percent to 30 percent.

More recently, Princeton sociologist Bruce Western mined NLSY data to show that incarceration has "large and enduring effects on job-prospects of ex-convicts." He found that the negative labor market effects of youth incarceration can last for more than a decade and that adult incarceration reduces paid employment by five to ten weeks annually. Because incarceration rates are especially high among those with the least power in the labor market (young and unskilled minority men), the U.S. justice system exacerbates inequality.

This research is consistent with numerous experimental studies suggesting that the employment prospects of job applicants with criminal records are far worse than the chances of persons who have never been convicted or imprisoned. It is consistent also with evidence from labor market intermediaries dealing with ex-offenders. Project STRIVE, an estab-

Toles. © 2000 by *The Buffalo News*. Reproduced by permission.

lished job-placement program that mainly serves younger minority males in inner-city Chicago, reports that it placed thirty-seven of fifty ex-offenders in jobs [in 2001], leaving a 26 percent unemployment rate even for people who went through an especially successful program. The Center for Employment Opportunity in New York City is another "successful" program. Focused specifically on ex-offenders, it fails to place nearly a third of its clients. Another standard bearer in the field, "Project Rio" of the Texas Workforce Commission, claims to process fifteen thousand inmates a year. After one year, a little over two-thirds of parolees who go through Project Rio hold jobs. More telling, since most ex-offenders are thrown into the labor market without the benefit of a transitional employment program, just 36 percent of a group of Texas parolees who did not enroll in Project Rio had a job one year after their release. And "even when paroled inmates are able to find jobs," the *New York Times* reported [in the fall of 2001], "they earn only half as much as people of the same social and economic background who have not been incarcerated."

The obstacles to ex-offender employment include the refusal of many employers even to consider hiring an "ex-con." Employers routinely check for criminal backgrounds in numerous sectors, including banking, security, financial services, law, education, and health care. But for many jobs, employer attitudes are irrelevant: state codes place steep barriers to the hiring of ex-offenders in numerous government and other occupations. At the same time, Western notes, "the increasingly violent and overcrowded state of prisons and jails is likely to produce certain attitudes, mannerisms, and behavioral practices that 'on the inside' function to enhance survival but are not compatible with success in the conventional job market." The alternately aggressive and sullen posture that prevails behind bars is deadly in a job market where entry-level occupations increasingly demand "soft" skills related to selling and customer service. In this as in countless other ways, the inmate may be removed, at least temporarily (see below), from prison, but prison lives on within the ex-offender, limiting his or her freedom on the outside.

A Vicious Circle

The situation arising from mass black incarceration is fraught with self-fulfilling policy ironies. At the very moment that American public discourse in racial matters has become officially inclusive, the United States is filling its expanding number of cellblocks with an ever-rising sea of black people monitored by predominantly white overseers. Echoes of slavery haunt the new incarceration state, reminding us of unresolved historical issues in the United States of Amnesia.

Mass incarceration is just as ironically juxtaposed to welfare reform. Even as the broader political and policy-making community is replacing taxpayer-financed "welfare dependency" with "workforce attachment" and free market discipline leading (supposedly) to "self-sufficiency" and two-parent family stability among the urban "underclass," criminal justice policies are pushing hundreds of thousands of already disadvantaged and impoverished blacks further from minimally remunerative engagement with the labor market. It does this by warehousing them in expensive, publicly financed, sex-segregated holding pens, where rehabilitation has been discredited and authoritarian incapacitation is the rule.

Droves of alienated men are removed from contact with children, parents, spouses, and lovers, contributing to the chronic shortage of suitable male marriage partners and resident fathers in the black community. Black humor on Chicago's South Side quips that "the only thing prison cures is heterosexuality." A connection probably exists between rampant sexual assault and sexual segregation behind prison bars and the disturbing fact that AIDS is now the leading cause of death among blacks between the ages of 25 and 44. Incarceration deepens a job-skill deficit that is a leading factor explaining "criminal" behavior among disadvantaged people in the first place. "Crime rates are inversely related," Richard B. Freeman and Jeffrey Fagan have shown, "to expected legal wages, particularly among young males with limited job skills or prospects." The "war on drugs" that contributes so strongly to minority incarceration also inflates the price of underground substances. Combined with ex-offenders' shortage of marketable skills in the legal economy, it creates irresistible incentives for the sort of income-generating conduct that leads back to prison. The lost potential earnings, savings, consumer demand, and human and social capital that result from mass incarceration cost black communities untold millions of dollars in potential economic development, worsening an inner-city political economy already crippled by decades of capital flight and de-industrialization. The dazed and embittered graduates of the prison-industrial complex are released back into a small number of predominantly black and high-poverty ZIP codes and census tracts, deepening the concentration of poverty, crime, and despair that is the hallmark of modern American "hyper-segregation" by race and class.

Meanwhile, prisoners' deletion from official U.S. unemployment statistics contributes to excessively rosy perceptions of American socioeconomic performance that worsen the political climate for minorities. Bruce Western has shown that factoring incarceration into unemployment rates challenges the conventional American notion that unregulated labor markets have been out-performing Europe's supposedly hyper-regulated employment system. Far from taking a laissez-faire approach, "the U.S. state has made a large and coercive intervention into the labor market through the expansion of the legal system." An American unemployment rate adjusted for imprisonment would rise by two points, bringing the U.S. ratio much closer to that of European nations, where including inmates raises the joblessness rate by only a few tenths of a percentage point. Counting prisoners would raise the official black male unemployment rate, which Western estimates at nearly 39 percent during the mid-1990s (including prisoners). Western and his colleague Becky Petit find that, when incarceration is factored in, there was "no enduring recovery in the employment of young black high-school drop-outs" during the eight-year Clinton employment boom.

By artificially reducing both aggregate and racially specific unemployment rates, mass incarceration makes it easier for the majority culture to continue to ignore the urban ghettoes that live on beneath official rhetoric about "opportunity" being generated by "free markets." It encourages and enables the new, that is, subtler and more covert racism. Relying heavily on longstanding American opportunity myths and standard class ideology, this new racism blames inner-city minorities for their own "failure" to match white performance in a supposedly now free, meritorious, and color-blind society. Whites who believe that racial barriers have been lifted in the United States think that people of color who do not "succeed" fall short because of choices they made or because of inherent cultural or even biological limitations.

Correctional Keynesianism

The ultimate policy irony at the heart of America's passion for prisons can be summarized by the phrase "correctional Keynesianism" [after economist John Maynard Keynes]: the prison construction boom fed by the rising market of black offenders is a job and tax-base creator for predominantly white communities that are generally far removed from urban minority concentrations. These communities, often recently hollowed out by the de-industrializing and family-farm-destroying gales of the "free market" system, have become part of a prison-industrial lobby that presses for harsher sentences and tougher laws, seeking to protect and expand their economic base even as crime rates continue to fall. They do so with good reason. The prison-building boom serves as what British sociologist David Ladipo calls "a latter-day Keynesian infrastructural investment program for [often] blight-struck communities. . . . Indeed, it has been phenomenally successful in terms of creating relatively secure, decent paid, and often unionized jobs."

According to Todd Clear, the negative labor market effects of mass incarceration on black communities are probably minor "compared to the economic relocation of resources" from black to white communities that mass incarceration entails. As Clear explains,

> Each prisoner represents an economic asset that has been removed from that community and placed elsewhere. As an economic being, the person would spend money at or near his or her area of residence—typically, an inner city. Imprisonment displaces that economic activity: Instead of buying snacks in a local deli, the prisoner makes those purchases in a prison commissary. The removal may represent a loss of economic value to the home community, but it is a boon to the prison [host] community. Each prisoner represents as much as $25,000 in income for the community in which the prison is located, not to mention the value of constructing the prison facility in the first place. This can be a massive transfer of value: A young male worth a few thousand dollars of support to children and local purchases is transformed into a $25,000 financial asset to a rural prison community. The economy of the rural community is artificially amplified, the local city economy artificially deflated. It's a disturbing picture, even in this cynical age, full of unsettling parallels and living links to chattel slavery: young black men being involuntarily removed as "economic assets" from black communities to distant rural destinations where they are kept under lock and key by white-majority overseers. It is difficult to imagine a more pathetic denouement to America's long, interwoven narratives of class and racial privilege. The rise of correctional Keynesianism is one of the negative and racially charged consequences of technically color-blind political-economic processes. . . .

To be sure, it is no simple matter to determine the precise extent to which mass incarceration is simply exacerbating the deep socioeconomic and related cultural and political traumas that already plague inner-city communities and help explain disproportionate black "criminality," arrest, and incarceration in the first place. Still, it is undeniable that the rush to incarcerate is having a profoundly negative effect on black communities. Equally undeniable is the fact that black incarceration rates reflect deep racial bias in the criminal justice system and the broader society. Do the cheerleaders of "get tough" crime and sentencing policy really believe that African-Americans deserve to suffer so disproportionately at the hands of the criminal justice system? There is a vast literature showing that structural, institutional, and cultural racism and severe segregation by race and class are leading causes of inner-city crime. Another considerable body of literature shows that blacks are victims of racial bias at every level of the criminal justice system—from stop, frisk, and arrest to prosecution, sentencing, release, and execution. These disparities give legitimacy to the movement of ex-offender groups for the expungement of criminal and prison records for many nonviolent offenses, especially in cases where ex-convicts have shown an earnest desire to go straight.

Further and deeper remedies are required. These include a moratorium on new prison construction (to stop the insidious, self-replicating expansion of the prison-industrial complex), the repeal of laws that deny voting rights to felons and ex-felons; amnesty and release for most inmates convicted of nonviolent crimes; decriminalization of narcotics; the repeal of the "war on drugs" at home and abroad; revision of state and federal sentencing and local "zero tolerance" practices and ordinances; abolition of racial, ethnic and class profiling in police practice; and the outlawing of private, for-profit prisons and other economic activities that derive investment gain from mass incarceration. Activists and policy makers should call for a criminal- to social-justice peace dividend: the large-scale transfer of funds spent on mass arrest, surveillance and incarceration into such policy areas as drug treatment, job-training, transitional services for ex-offenders and public education regarding the employment potential of ex-offenders. They should call for the diversion of criminal justice resources from crime in the streets (that is, the harassment and imprisonment of lower-class and inner-city people) to serious engagement with under-sentenced crime in the suites. More broadly, they should seek a general redistribution of resources from privileged and often fantastically wealthy persons to those most penalized from birth by America's inherited class and race privilege. America's expanding prison, probation and parole populations are recruited especially from what leading slavery reparations advocate Randall Robinson calls "the millions of African-Americans bottommired in urban hells by the savage time-release social debilitations of American slavery."

The ultimate solutions lie, perhaps, beyond the parameters of the existing political economic order. "Capitalism," Eugene Debs argued in 1920, "needs and must have the prison to protect itself from the [lower-class] criminals it has created." But the examples of Western Europe and Canada, where policy makers prefer prevention and rehabilitation through more social democratic approaches, show that mass incarceration is hardly an inevitable product of capitalism. And nothing can excuse policy makers and activists from the responsibility to end racist criminal justice practices that significantly exacerbate the difficulties faced by the nation's most disadvantaged. More than merely a symptom of the tangled mess of problems that create, sustain and deepen America's insidious patterns of class and race inequality, mass incarceration has become a central part of the mess. For these and other reasons, it will be an especially worthy target for creative democratic protest and policy formation in the new millennium.

"Blaming the criminal justice system, a bad economic situation, or racism for the high number of blacks in prison is a cheap cop out. Secular humanists, the media and black liberals are giving our black youth excuses for committing crimes."

The Prison System Is Not Racist

R.D. Davis

R.D. Davis is a member of the African American leadership network Project 21, a writer, and a radio talk show host in Huntsville, Alabama. In this viewpoint Davis challenges the view that racism explains why U.S. prisons hold a disproportionate number of blacks. He contends that prisons house more minorities because they commit a disproportionately high number of crimes. Davis also refutes the suggestion by some critics that it is poverty that drives crime and fills the prisons with black offenders, pointing out that more white people than blacks are poor.

As you read, consider the following questions:
1. What percentage of murders in America are committed by blacks, according to statistics Davis cites?
2. Who does Davis consider to be the real victims of black crime?
3. Which groups does Davis accuse of providing black youth excuses for committing crimes?

Racism is blamed for just about everything negative involving blacks. The debilitating effect of this is that it doen't afford us the motivation to look inward and work to find effective solutions to our race's problems. It's easier to just holler "Hey, look over yonder" than look right here.

That's what is happening with the implication that racism is the reason for the disproportionate number of blacks in prison. Those who consider the fact that one-half of the murders in America are committed by blacks (mostly male and black-on-black) could easily conclude that blacks commit disproportionately high rates of other types of crime. Notice that bars also guard homes, businesses and even churches in some of our neighborhoods. Those who are suffering are law-abiding, poor blacks who cannot afford to escape those crime-infested neighborhoods. But the media and our so-called black leaders seem to be more concerned about the welfare of black criminals than about the safety of average citizens.

A good example of this attitude was featured in an article that appeared on the front page of *The Huntsville Times.* The article noted that two out of three Alabamans in prison are black although almost three out of every four Alabamans are white.

A Moral, Not a Racial Issue

Racism, of course, must be the culprit. After all, what else could it possibly be? State Representative Alvin Holmes, a black Democrat, said the numbers were "shocking and unbelievable." He added, "It makes you wonder, as a person who went to jail 27 times for civil rights causes, if your work was in vain and worth the suffering you went through."

Am I missing something here? As someone who has read several books on Dr. Martin Luther King, Jr. and the civil rights movement, I don't remember anyone in the past fighting for the civil rights of hardened criminals of any race. Besides, why are we demonizing the criminal justice system instead of those who commit the crimes? After all, the law-abiding citizens whom the crimes are perpetrated against are the victims, not the criminals. Moreover, I think this is a moral issue rather than a racial one. Can I hear some

Not Racist, Just Indifferent

Why, if our sentences are so harsh, has there not been more of a public outcry. To a large extent the answer is found in the population upon whom we are imposing these harsh and cruel sentences. Of the 151,000 prisoners in our federal prisons today, 40% are Black, 32% are Hispanic, another 3% are Asian or Native American.

While there may be some overlap in the Black and Hispanic populations, I think it is fair to estimate that between 65 and 70% of the federal prison population are minorities. I do not believe that we have a consciously racist criminal justice system. I do believe, however, that, because these sentences are imposed on minorities, they do not cause the majority community the concern they would feel, if the defendants were people with whom we identified in a meaningful way. Several years ago in a speech to the Federal Bar Council in New York, my former colleague, Bob Carter said that if as large a percentage of the White community was being imprisoned as is happening in the Black community, our society simply would not tolerate it and would look more closely at the root causes and do something. I am firmly convinced he is correct. It is not that we are consciously trying to imprison minorities, we simply do not care enough about the problems that minorities face.

John S. Martin Jr., "Cruel and Too Usual—Sentencing in the Federal Courts," October 31, 2003.

amens from the ministers out there?

The *Times* reported that the director of Auburn University's Montgomery Center for Demographic Research, Don Bogie, said the prison statistics prove there are problems in the state's legal system. "It gives an indication that they are going after the kinds of crimes that are committed by people of lower incomes," said Bogie.

Economics Not to Blame

Robert Sigler, a criminal justice professor at the University of Alabama, "theorizes" the reasons are more economic than racial. "Poor people go to prison. People of wealth don't," Sigler said, adding, "A large number of black Americans are poor." Now I'm really confused. When the debate is "blacks on welfare," the comeback is inevitably "there are more whites on welfare." In "raw" numbers, this is true. But if poor whites outnumber poor blacks in America, and being poor is the only reason for the disparity behind bars, then please tell me why there aren't more (poor) whites in prison than (poor) blacks. Jeeeez!

State Representative Holmes agreed with Sigler. "Economics—that's 99 percent of it," Holmes said. "When people are unemployed, they are hungry. The water is off. The lights are off. It causes them to do things that people who are employed with money don't do." This is garbage. I will venture to say that the majority of poor blacks who fall in this dismal economic category are law-abiding and God-fearing, moral people who don't look to crime as a solution. Holmes also says this leaves less than one percent of the problem to drug abuse and other factors. This is unrealistic. And I guess the fact that the majority of the blacks in prisons are fatherless also has nothing to do with their situation.

Blaming the criminal justice system, a bad economic situation, or racism for the high number of blacks in prison is a cheap cop-out. Secular humanists, the media and black liberals are giving our black youth excuses for committing crimes. They won't admit the high number of blacks in prison is a moral issue. Neither would they admonish the advice "If you don't want to do the time, don't do the crime." No, that would be too simple.

"Correctional bureaucrats have devised a systematically humiliating and, indeed, dehumanizing regimen of punishments for prisoners who elsewhere would more likely be considered disturbed."

Supermaximum Security Prisons Are Cruel

Sasha Abramsky

Sasha Abramsky is a freelance journalist and author of *Hard Time Blues: How Politics Built a Prison Nation.* In this viewpoint he concedes that although supermax prisons, in which violent and disruptive prisoners are kept in solitary confinement, may be a necesary last resort for "the worst of the worst" prisoners, evidence shows that overuse of the facilities to hold less troublesome inmates is common. According to psychiatric testimony reported by the author, the sensory deprivation of supermax confinement has resulted in extreme manifestation of phychosis in some inmates. The long-term spells of deprivation and isolation have made many prisoners more violent, putting society at risk when the prisoners are released, Abramsky claims.

As you read, consider the following questions:

1. In Abramsky's view, what circumstances led to the development of supermax prisons?
2. Have supermax prisons reduced the level of prisoner violence, according to the author?
3. As reported by Abramsky, is mental health treatment of supermax inmates adequate?

The supermax model emerged out of the prison violence of the 1970s and the early 1980s, when dozens of guards around the country, including two at the maximum-security federal prison at Marion, Illinois, were murdered by prisoners. First, prison authorities developed procedures to minimize inmate-staff contact; then they took to "locking down" entire prisons for indefinite periods, keeping inmates in their cells all day and closing down communal dining rooms and exercise yards. Eventually, they began to explore the idea of making the general prison population safer by creating entirely separate high-tech, supermax prisons in which the "worst of the worst" gang leaders and sociopaths would be incarcerated in permanent lockdown conditions. In the late 1980s, several states and the federal government began constructing supermax units. California—which had seen 11 guards murdered by inmates between 1970 and 1973, and a staggering 32 prisoners killed by other inmates in 1972 alone—opened Corcoran State Prison and its super-max unit in 1968 and Pelican Bay the year following. In 1994 the first federal supermax opened, in Florence, Colorado. Soon, dozens of correctional systems across the country were embracing this model.

Indeed, throughout the 1990s, despite year-by-year declines in crime, one state after another pumped tens of millions of dollars into building supermax prisons and supermax facilities within existing prisons—sections that are usually called "secure housing units," or SHUs. Defenders of supermaxes, like Todd Ishea, warden of Ohio State Penitentiary (OSP), a supermax in Youngstown, argue that their restrictions provide a way to establish control in what is still—and inherently—an extremely dangerous environment. "In 1993," he says, "our maximum security prison at Southern Ohio Correctional Facility was host to a riot. One correctional officer was killed. A number of inmates were killed and several injured. Following the riot, the department made a decision that a 500-bed facility of this nature was needed to control the most dangerous inmates."

Casual Overuse Common

But while it may be necessary to maintain such restricted facilities as prisons of last resort for some inmates, critics point out that far less troublesome inmates end up being sent to them. In Ohio, for example, a special legislative committee appointed to inspect the state's prisons in 1999 concluded that fewer than half of the inmates at OSP met the state's own supermax guidelines. State correctional-department data indicate that of the more than 350 inmates currently incarcerated at OSP, 20 were ringleaders of the 1993 riot and 31 had killed either an inmate or a correctional officer while living among the general prison population; but the rest had been sent there for much less serious offenses (often little more than a fistfight with another inmate).

State Torture Chamber

Pelican Bay State Torture Chamber is located in one of the most beautiful areas of California, close to the Pacific Ocean and near redwood forests. Three square miles of trees were clear-cut to build a humongous torture chamber to encage 1,500 human beings. What evil-minded people thought up this one?!—killing trees to build a structure to torture human beings for years!

The prisoners in [Pelican Bay Supermax Prison] can't see trees, nor the sun nor clouds nor rain nor hear birds. They are totally shut off from the beautiful nature that surrounds them. The entire prison area sits on gravel; not even token blades of grass or weeds can be seen. Three sets of fences surround the prison. Two fences are chain link with curled up barbed wire at the top. Sandwiched in between these two fences is an electrified fence that kills you on contact. I wouldn't wish my worst enemy to be encaged in such a place.

Donna Wallach, "A Visit to Pelican Bay State Torture Chamber," *San Francisco Bay View*. www.sfbayview.com, October 30, 2002.

And Ohio isn't alone in this practice. According to a study issued by the state of Florida, fully one-third of the correctional departments across the country that operate supermax prisons report placing inmates in them simply because they don't have enough short-term disciplinary housing in lower-security prisons. Given that the supermaxes' average cost to taxpayers is about $50,000 per inmate per year—compared with $20,000 to $30,000 for lower-security prisons—this is hardly an economically efficient arrangement.

Yet the available numbers suggest that casual overuse of

these facilities is common. For in tough-on-crime America, imposing grim conditions on prisoners is all too often seen as a good in itself, regardless of the long-term costs. The U.S. Department of Justice's 1997 report on supermax housing . . . found Mississippi officials insisting that they needed to house fully 20 percent of their prison inmates in separate supermax-type prisons and another 35 percent in similar units within existing prisons. Arizona claimed that it needed to house 8 percent of its inmates in supermax prisons and another 20 percent in SHUs. In Virginia, after Jim Austin, the state's nationally renowned consultant on prisoner classification, told officials that they needed to put more of their inmates into medium-security prisons, the state instead spent approximately $150 million to build Red Onion and Wallens Ridge, two supermax prisons with a combined capacity to house 2,400 prisoners.

Psychiatric Disorders

Proponents of the supermax system claim that its introduction has reduced violence in the general prison population—both by removing the most hard-core miscreants and introducing a fearsome deterrent to misbehavior. But the data on this are, at best, mixed. Among Ohio's total prison population, for example, there were more inmate-on-inmate assults serious enough to be written up by officials in 2000 than there were in 1997, the year before the OSP supermax opened for business (8 assaults for every 1,000 prisoners in 1997 compared with 10 for every 1,000 in 2000). And even where lower-security prisons have been made somewhat safer, that safety has been purchased at a staggering financial and, ultimately, social cost.

Even the best-run of the supermax facilities seem to see high rates of mental illness among their inmates. For example, a study carried out by the Washington State Department of Corrections, which is known as one of the more humane, rehabilitation-focused prison systems in the country, found that approximately 30 percent of inmates in its supermax units show evidence of serious psychiatric disorders—at least twice the rate in the overall prison population. . . .

The greatly disputed chicken-and-egg question is: Do

previously healthy inmates go mad under these extreme conditions of confinement, or do inmates who are already mentally unstable and impulsive commit disciplinary infractions that get them shipped off to SHUs or supermax prisons, where they are then likely to further decompensate?

Some psychiatrists, including Harvard University professor Stuart Grassian, have testified in court that the sensory deprivation in a supermax frequently leads otherwise healthy individuals to develop extreme manifestations of psychosis, such as hallucinations, uncontrollable rage, paranoia, and nearly catatonic depressions. Grassian and others have also documented examples of extreme self-mutilation: supermax inmates gouging out their eyes or cutting off their genitals. Using the tools of the supermax prison, writes James Gilligan in his book *Violence*, "does not protect the public; it only sends a human time bomb into the community" when the inmate is eventually released.

Minimal Mental Health Treatment

Other psychiatrists are more cautious, arguing that while some perfectly healthy people are driven insane by these dehumanizing prison settings, the more common problem is that mildly mentally ill inmates are often precisely the ones who find it hardest to control their behavior while in the general prison population and who therefore get sent to the supermax or SHU. [U.S. District Court] Judge [Thelton] Henderson acknowledged this in his Pelican Bay ruling; and in *Ruiz v. Johnson*, a 1999 case involving Texas's use of long-term inmate-segregation facilities in its prisons, another federal court likewise found that "inmates, obviously in need of medical help, are instead inappropriately managed merely as miscreants."

In the large supermaxes of Texas, correctional bureaucrats have devised a systematically humiliating and, indeed, dehumanizing regimen of punishments for prisoners who elsewhere would more likely be considered disturbed: no real meals, only a "food loaf" of all the day's food ground together, for prisoners who don't return their food trays; paper gowns forced on those who won't wear their clothes. I myself have heard guards joking about "the mutilators" who slash their own veins to get attention. According to Thomas Conkin, a psychiatrist and medical director at the Hampden County Jail in Massachusetts who was called on to evaluate mental-health care in one Texas supermax. "All suicide gestures by inmates [were] seen as manipulating the correctional system with the conscious intent of secondary gain. In not one case was the inmate's behavior seen as reflecting mental pathology that could be treated." In most supermaxes, this kind of thinking still seems to be the norm.

Although prison authorities say that they provide mental-health care to their supermax inmates, prisoner advocates tend to dismiss these claims. Documentary-film maker Jim Lipscomb, who has interviewed scores of inmates in Ohio's most secure prisons, reports that mental-health programs there often consist of little more than in-cell videos offering such platitudes as "if you feel angry at one of the guards, try not to curse and shout at him."

"That's called mental health!" Lipscomb says in amazement. . . .

Supermax Prisons Breed Violence

Tens of thousands of inmates are now being held in supermax facilities, and almost all of them will be released one day. Indeed, many states are releasing such inmates directly from the SHUs to the streets after their sentence is up, without even reacclimatizing them to a social environment.

Although no national tracking surveys of ex-supermax and ex-SHU inmates have been carried out, anecdotal evidence suggests that many prisoners have been made more violent by their long-term spells of extreme deprivation and isolation. Bonnie Kerness of the AFSC [American Friends Service Committee] talks about a whole new generation of cons coming out of supermax prisons with hair-trigger tempers. One former inmate at Rikers Island jail in New York City, who now participates in a rehabilitation program run by the Manhattan-based Fortune Society, recalls that prisoners routinely referred to "Bing monsters." (The Bing is the nickname for the Rikers Island version of the SHU.)

"The impact on society could be devastating," says Steve Rigg, a former correctional officer who worked at California's supermax prison in Corcoran during the mid-1990s and blew the whistle on his fellow officers for organizing fights between rival prison-gang members. Corcoran's administration was overhauled after this, but Rigg warns that the underlying dangers in undermonitored supermaxes remain. "There's more [inmate] recidivism," he says of SHUs. "They breed the worst."

"The overriding justification for the use of a supermax philosophy is rooted in the need for security."

Supermaximum Security Prisons Are Necessary

Thomas J. Stickrath and Gregory A. Bucholtz

Thomas J. Stickrath and Gregory A. Bucholtz are corrections professionals with the Ohio Department of Rehabilitation and Correction. Stickrath is the assistant director of the department and Bucholtz is an assistant chief inspector. In this viewpoint they contend that supermax prisons are essential to maintaining institutional safety and security for prison staff and inmates. They argue that the existence of supermax prisons, where violent and disruptive inmates go to spend time in solitary confinement, also serves as a deterrent to violent and seriously disruptive inmate behavior.

As you read, consider the following questions:

1. What two reasons do Stickrath and Bucholtz cite for the proliferation of supermax prisons in America?
2. What are some inmate behaviors that could land an inmate in supermax isolation, according to the authors?
3. As reported by the authors, how long do inmates remain in supermax isolation? Who determines when they are released into the general prison population?

M any states have housed their most violent inmates in one or more prisons, but they have seldom operated routinely on total lockdown. Even maximum-security prisons usually allow inmate movement, interaction, and work. Today, however, most of the sixty or more supermax prisons in operation in the United States use the total lockdown philosophy as a method of controlling today's violent and disruptive inmates.

The reasons for the proliferation of supermax prisons in America are twofold. First, many correctional systems have been confronted with crowding due to the increasing inmate population and the influx of drug offenders, gang members, mentally ill, and young offenders. To maintain order, these systems have chosen to isolate the most disruptive inmates from the general population. Some officials state that their supermax prisons also act as a deterrent for some offenders who might be prone to disruptive behavior.

Second, supermax prisons are politically and publicly attractive. They are symbols that a state is getting "tough on crime.". . .

Special Management Housing

The types of behavior constituting potential assignment into a lockdown environment such as a special management housing unit or supermax facility is strikingly similar across all states. Despite a wide variance between jurisdictions on the definition of supermax, most use similar, specific behaviors and types of associations when recommending inmate placements into supermax confinement.

Criteria for placement consideration generally include: committing violent assaults against staff and other offenders, making a serious escape threat, being a gang leader or enforcer, and trying to have substantial quantities of drugs smuggled or conveyed into a prison. In some states, such as Virginia, sentence length also is taken into account. The criteria used by correctional systems are presented only as a guideline for use in determining the most appropriate inmate classification assignments.

A small number of inmates may exhibit behavior that has an impact directly and/or indirectly on the stability of opera-

One Definition of Supermax Housing

A freestanding facility, or a distinct unit within a facility, that provides for the management and secure control of inmates who have been officially designated as exhibiting violent or seriously disruptive behavior while incarcerated. Such inmates have been determined to be a threat to safety and security in traditional high-security facilities, and only separation, restricted movement, and limited direct access to staff and other inmates can control their behavior.

National Institute of Corrections, 1997.

tions. Therefore, the potential risk lends support for separating the inmates from the general population. In fact, it could be argued that this concept has been the premise for segregation units since their inception. When particular behaviors threaten the very fabric of a facility's security, then the facility must attempt to reestablish the parameters governing its correctional management. Traditionally, jurisdictions have generally addressed the problem by using special management or housing units that isolate inmates for a definite period of time spanning either a couple of days or several months. By design, these units are located within the existing facility where the behavior occurred. Spatial differentiation from the general population, thereby, is minimal. . . .

Operational Security

The overriding justification for the use of a supermax philosophy is rooted in the need for security. In virtually every case, inmate placement into this type of environment has rested on past behaviors, either "on the street" or during their incarceration. Actual disruptive behavior, however, may not necessarily identify those inmates most threatening to the safety and security of an institution. Take, for example, a known prison gang leader who may have a "clean" conduct report history but who instructs others to commit violations. For traditional classification systems (which contain either static or dynamic/changeable) measures of inmate behavior, the gang leader most likely will score at a decreased security level despite being a serious security threat. Actual behavior, therefore, cannot in and of itself be the lone criteria for determining whether a particular inmate is a risk to security.

Sometimes, intelligence gathered both internally and externally to the correctional system helps identify inmates for supermax placement. Internally, security threat group teams, telephone and mail monitoring, and inmate informants are used to prevent potential security problems. External intelligence gathered sometimes also can result in a temporary supermax placement for inmates. Other criminal justice organizations, such as law enforcement, prosecutors, and judges, often provide correctional departments with information that indicates particular inmates present a danger to security. . . .

Security Reduction

Inmates classified into a supermax environment usually remain in that status for an indefinite period of time. Although inmates in this status are periodically evaluated for reclassification purposes, decisions on security reductions are usually based on the professional judgment of staff, which involves a determination as to whether the inmates no longer represent a high level of threat to security. In order to progress out of supermax confinement, inmates generally must move through a graduated system of levels (Ohio) or housing units (ADX Florence) based on institutional conduct and adherence to individual program and behavior plans. . . .

With public sentiment continuing to promote a tough-on-crime mindset, corrections will remain a primary focus of state and federal legislatures. However, as the field of corrections is forced to become more fiscally accountable for the increasing costs of incarceration, the spotlight will continue to focus on the need for supermax prisons.

"Abuse will not end until states and counties and the federal government start passing strict laws limiting contact between male correctional officers and female inmates."

Cross-Gender Prisoner Searches Are Abusive

Alan Elsner

Alan Elsner is a national correspondent for Reuters and author of the book *Gates of Injustice: The Crisis in America's Prisons.* In this viewpoint Elsner contends that the presence of male correctional officers in women's prisons and jails contributes to the rampant abuse of women prisoners in America. For example, the author argues that male officers, when given the opportunity, may disregard prison procedures during a search and fondle female inmates. When sexual misconduct occurs, Elsner contends, prisoners are often afraid to complain.

As you read, consider the following questions:

1. What percentage of male correctional officers works with female prisoners, as reported by Elsner?
2. What laws does the author cite that eliminated many restrictions on the role of male guards in women's prisons?
3. According to the author, why were lawsuits brought to assure "gender neutral" employment policies in U.S. prisons?

Alan Elsner, "Jailed Women's Abuse Is National Scandal," *Women's eNews*, April 14, 2004. Copyright © 2004 by *Women's eNews*. Reproduced by permission.

Sixteen months after a judge ordered Alabama to end horrific conditions and abuse at the state's Julia Tutwiler Prison for Women, information that emerged [in April 2004] shows that, for some inmates, the suffering has only gotten worse.

In December 2002, U.S. District Court Judge Myron Thompson found that Tutwiler inmates were held in large dormitories, hundreds squashed together in unventilated rooms with nothing to do all day. Over 1,000 inmates occupied a facility originally built to house 364. The summer heat was stifling but there were not enough fans to cover all the dorms. Violence among inmates was common; health care was so inadequate that it bordered on the criminally negligent.

Thompson ordered the state to reduce overcrowding and in 2003 Alabama shipped 300 inmates to the South Louisiana Correctional Center, a private prison in Louisiana to comply with the order. Last week [April 2004], *The Birmingham News* reported that the Evangeline Parish District Attorney Brent Coreil would pursue criminal charges against an unspecified number of guards accused of improper sexual contact with the prisoners.

Also last week, Livingston County in Michigan settled a class-action lawsuit brought by 233 former inmates of the county jail for $355,000. They alleged, among other things, that male guards watched them take showers and use the toilet and denied them feminine hygiene products.

Exposing Rampant Abuse

These cases shine a light on the rampant abuse that many of the 180,000 women in our nation's prisons and jails risk every day. The problem of male correctional officers sexually harassing, abusing and raping female inmates permeates our nation's prisons and jails.

Women entering U.S. prisons and jails stand a good chance of being guarded by male correctional officers. A 1997 survey of prisons in 40 states found that on average 41 percent of the correctional officers working with female inmates were men. Two-thirds of those guarding women in California were men; in Kansas, the figure was 72 percent.

In the past, the role of male guards in women's prisons was restricted to functions that limited actual physical contact. Civil rights and anti-discrimination laws passed since the 1960s swept many of these restrictions away. Ironically, this was partly a result of lawsuits launched by female corrections officers to win the right to work in men's prisons. States responded by writing "gender neutral" employment policies. But women often do not receive gender-neutral treatment.

Sexual Abuse of Women in Prison

International guardians of human rights Amnesty International, Human Rights Watch, and the United Nations Special Commission on Violence Against Women, have condemned United States prisons for the existence of prevalent sexual abuse of female inmates by correctional staff. Much of the trouble stems from the fact that many existing prisons in the United States are in violation of international standards of the United Nations Standard Minimum Rules for the Treatment of Prisoners which forbid male guards to supervise women's prisons. A 1997 study of forty states found that, on average, 41 percent of officers at women's prisons are men.

In many states, male guards have the legal right to touch female inmates anywhere on their bodies (including their breasts and genitals) when conducting searches and to observe them using the toilets and showers. The ultimate authority of male officers over female inmates creates a situation ripe for abuse. The sexual abuse documented in U.S. prisons ranges from sexually suggestive statements, to prurient viewing, to groping, to rape.

According to the International Covenant on Civil and Political Rights, sexual abuse violates both the right to be treated with respect for human dignity and the right to privacy—two rights to which all human beings are entitled. And the rape of an inmate by prison staff is considered, under international law, an act of torture.

"Women in Prison" Agenda Publications, LLC. www.personal.umich.edu, July/August 2002.

For several years throughout the 1990s, officials at the Suffolk County Jail in Boston routinely strip-searched every single woman booked into the facility; over 5,400 women in total. This policy was for women only. Male pre-arraignment detainees were held in a Boston police lock-up and were not automatically strip-searched.

Limits on Male Supervision

Prisons in different states are still searching for an answer to the question: What, if any, limits should be placed on male officers supervising female inmates? Take the issue of prison "pat-downs" where male guards frisk female inmates through their clothes. In one 1993 case, decided by the U.S. Court of Appeals for the Ninth Circuit, Judge Diarmuid O'Scannlain described how such a search was conducted.

"During the cross-gender clothed body search, the male guard stands next to the female inmate and thoroughly runs his hands over her clothed body starting with her neck and working down to her feet. According to the prison training material, the guard is to 'use a flat hand and pushing motion across the (inmate's) crotch area.' The guard must 'push inward and upward when searching the crotch and upper thighs of the inmate.' All seams in the leg and the crotch area are to be 'squeezed and kneaded.' Using the back of the hand, the guard also is to search the breast area in a sweeping motion, so that the breasts will be 'flattened.'"

That was a search conducted by the book. But can there possibly be any doubt that many officers disregard procedures and take the opportunity to grope or fondle the women they are searching?

In a 2003 class-action suit, a group of prisoners in New York described how officers stroked their breasts, grabbed their crotches and made sexual or obscene comments while they were conducting searches. It may be a minority of officers but when the temptation is so manifestly there, when the person doing the searching has all the power and the person being searched has none, some guards will abuse their authority.

Afraid to Complain

In many cases of sexual misconduct, prisoners are afraid to complain. If there is no medical or physical evidence and no witnesses, allegations come down to "he said, she said" situations. An inmate's word is never as good as an officer's and both sides know this. Guards tell their victims, "Who are they going to believe? I have a badge and a uniform and you are a convicted criminal."

Often, sexual relationships in prisons have the outward appearance of consensual sex. Typically, a male officer grants favors to a female inmate in exchange for sex. Nobody ever complains and no reports are written. Both parties, it could be argued, get something out of the relationship.

In fact, this kind of relationship is no different from the sex between a slave owner and a bondwoman. This kind of abuse will not end until states and counties and the federal government start passing strict laws limiting contact between male correctional officers and female inmates. Until that time, women in our prisons and jails will continue to be victimized.

*"Cross-gender search and supervision
policies and procedures should address and
balance competing interests. The 'test of
reasonableness under the Fourth
Amendment . . . requires a balancing of
the need for the particular search against
the invasion of personal rights that the
search entails.'"*

Cross-Gender Prisoner
Searches Can Be Justified

Gary W. DeLand

Gary W. DeLand is an author and criminal justice consultant.
In the following viewpoint he argues that when courts have
had to decide the legality of cross-gender searches, they have
had to weigh inmates' privacy rights against prisons' security
needs. According to DeLand, the courts have usually decided
that female searches of male inmates do not infringe on prisoners' privacy rights unduly. However, male searches of female prisoners are more often seen as violating prisoners'
rights because women often have a history of sexual abuse and
may react more negatively to cross-gender searches than
would men. Nonetheless, Leland points out, if prisons prove
a need for such searches, the courts will allow them.

As you read, consider the following questions:
1. As cited by DeLand, what constitutes a "reasonable
   accommodation" of prisoners' sexual privacy interests?
2. Do the security needs of a penal institution override an
   inmates' right to privacy, as reported by the author?

Gary W. DeLand, "Prisoner's Sexual Privacy Interests," www.justicetraining.com,
July 11, 2005. Copyright © 2005 by Gary W. DeLand. Reproduced by permission.

Courts have not been in complete agreement as to whether prisoners have sexual privacy interests, and if they do, the extent of such interests.

Some courts have taken the position that prisoners have little or no lawful expectation of sexual privacy. . . .

Other courts have recognized that, in fact, some right to sexual privacy exists for prisoners. . . .

Reasonable Accommodation

Cross-gender search and supervision policies and procedures should address and balance competing interests. The "test of reasonableness under the Fourth Amendment . . . requires a balancing of the need for the particular search against the invasion of personal rights that the search entails." "Although inmates' right to privacy must yield to the penal institution's need to maintain security . . ." [*Bell vs. Wolfish*].

Policies and procedures should ensure reasonable accommodation by officials. However, accommodation should not undermine the facility's legitimate safety and accuracy interests.

Reasonable accommodation may include:

1. assigning officers to posts which do not involve frequent or close observation of prisoners of the opposite sex;
2. providing modesty screens in front of toilets, showers, and drying areas;
3. adjusting staff post assignments and schedules; or
4. having officers of opposite sex announce that they are on the block.

Caution should be exercised, however, in determining the extent to which corrections officials should accommodate prisoner's interests to avoid compromising vital security interests. For example:

1. announcing that an officer of the opposite sex is about to begin a surveillance round would destroy the element of surprise and greatly reduce the effectiveness of surveillance rounds; and
2. "Covering the shower area [to prevent female officers from seeing prisoners while showering] would cut down on the guards' abilities to determine whether an assault

had occurred in the showers . . . [and] would enhance the possibilities of such assaults" [*Johnson vs. Pennsylvania Department of Corrections*].

Prisoners must also make reasonable accommodations of their own if they wish to protect their modesty. Prisoners can for example:

1. reduce intrusion by adjusting their own habits; and
2. protect sexual privacy by "covering himself while sitting on toilet" [*Bagley vs. Watson*].

Professional conduct by officers will go a long way toward establishing the reasonableness of cross-gender searches and supervision and is particularly important in sustaining cross-gender searches against constitutional challenges.

Female Searches of Males

Personal searches, though an intrusion on the sexual privacy of prisoners, when performed properly are neither unreasonable nor unconstitutional when performed by persons of the same gender. The question is whether searches by officers of the opposite sex of the subject being searched remain constitutional.

Frisk and rub searches are not ordinarily considered to be highly intrusive searches, but when such searches of male prisoners are performed by women they are considered to be more intrusive. . . .

As a general rule the courts have supported policies permitting women to conduct searches of male prisoners which require touching.

The courts have varied significantly in their rulings on the scope or level of intrusion permitted in cross-gender frisk searches.

Some courts have permitted female officers essentially the same latitude in searching male prisoners as that allowed for male officers, while other courts have been more sympathetic to sexual privacy interests.

Other court rulings have affirmed female officers' searches conducted in a more limited manner. Some of these rulings approved incidental contact with genitals, but did not address the question of more direct rubbing.

Strip searches and VBC [Visual Body-Cavity] searches

Security Needs

It is generally accepted that prison inmates have some degree of freedom from visual exposure of and physical contact with their bodies. However, whatever rights the inmates have must be balanced against the legitimate needs and interests of the prison authorities, which primarily involve the maintenance of security for both prison staff and inmates and the goal of rehabilitation of inmates.

Courts uniformly recognize that observation and search of inmates are necessary to prevent the obtaining and the possession of weapons, drugs, and other contraband by inmates. Disagreement arises, however, as to the level of observation and search that is necessary and as to whether guards of the opposite gender may participate. Most courts give considerable deference to the experience and expertise of prison officials in these matters, as long as there is a rational basis for the procedures employed at the prison.

John Dwight Ingram, "Prison Guards and Inmates of Opposite Genders: Equal Employment Opportunity Versus Right of Privacy." www.law.duke.edu, 2000.

---

are more intrusive than frisk/rub searches. The intrusiveness is enhanced if done by an officer of the opposite sex.

Some courts have determined that there is no constitutional right to sexual privacy, or have found at best a restricted right. . . .

Even those courts which have restricted such searches provide exceptions to permit cross-gender searches when there are:

1. exigent circumstances or
2. voluntary exposures.

Male Searches of Females

A. General

There are significant differences between how the courts view female-on-male searches and male-on-female searches.

What's good for the goose is NOT good for the gander!!

1. Courts ruling that women can search male prisoners often make a specific point of disclaiming any application of the decision to male-on-female searches.
2. Various justifications have been used by courts in disal-

lowing male officer searches of female prisoners, despite permitting female officer searches of male prisoners.

- "There are cultural taboos in our society which prohibit men from touching women's breast and genital areas without consent."
- There are psychological and emotional differences between males and females which may cause female prisoners to react differently to cross-gender searches than would male prisoners.
- A substantial number of female prisoners have during their lifetime been victims of sexual assaults and other abuse by men, while it is extremely rare that female-on-male sexual assaults occur.
- Courts have also expressed concerns over the unique problems associated with men supervising or participating in searches of women prisoners experiencing menstruation or other "female problems."

B. *Rub/Frisk Searches*
1. There are very few cases involving male searches of female prisoners; probably a result of jail and prison policies prohibiting or greatly limiting male rub and frisk searches of female prisoners.
2. In a Washington case which did deal with the issue, after concluding that so-called "pet" searches were actually "rubbing," "kneading" searches, found unconstitutional on 8th Amendment grounds, routine and random rub searches of female prisoners by male officers.
3. While routine or random searches were struck down, some courts have permitted limited exceptions to the general prohibition against cross-gender rub searches of females when exigent circumstances or voluntary exposure occurs.

C. *Strip and Body Cavity Searches*
1. For many of the same reasons listed related to rub searches, courts are more protective of female's sexual privacy than of the privacy interests of male prisoners regarding strip searches of females by male officers.
2. There is no support in the law for routine or random cross-gender strip searches of female prisoners; however, some limited exceptions are recognized by courts.

3. The burden will be on staff to provide acceptable justification for any exceptions to the general rule. For example, in a 4th Circuit case, officers were liable when they were unable to justify their continued presence and assistance when a female prisoner agreed to change into suicide-prevention attire. Although upholding a later search where facts demonstrated exigent circumstances and a voluntary exposure of the prisoner's naked body, the jury awarded damages to a female prisoner whose clothing was forcibly removed after agreeing to remove her own clothing if the male officers would withdraw: . . . it was wholly unnecessary for the male guards to remain in the room and to restrain the plaintiff while her underclothing was forcefully removed [the court decided].

Periodical Bibliography

The following articles have been selected to supplement the diverse views presented in this chapter.

Joseph R. Biden Jr. and Orrin G. Hatch	"Pinstripes, Jail Stripes," *Philadelphia Inquirer,* July 9, 2002.
Rose Braz	"More than Just a Few 'Bad Apples': Confronting Prison Problems in Iraq, and in the U.S.," *RESIST,* July/August 2004.
Linda Chavez	"What Will It Take to Finally Protect Our Kids?" *Human Events,* July 8, 2005. www.humaneventsonline.com.
Cynthia Cooper	"A Cancer Grows: Medical Treatment in Women's Prisons Ranges from Brutal to Nonexistent," *Nation,* May 6, 2002.
Deborah Davies	"Torture in America's Brutal Prisons," *Channel 4 Dispatches,* March 2, 2005. www.information clearinghouse.info.
Detroit News	"Protect Female Prisoners from Male Prison Guards," January 30, 2005. www.detnews.com.
Judy Freyermuth	"Education in the DOJ's Bureau of Prisons: Rhetoric or Reality?" *Watching Justice,* July 20, 2004. www.watchingjustice.org.
Regan Good	"The Supermax Solution," *Nation,* March 3, 2003.
John Hawkins	"Put Career Criminals in Jail and Throw Away the Key," *Right Wing News,* July 18, 2003. www.rightwingnews.com.
Jeff Jacoby	"More Prisoners, Less Crime," *Boston Globe,* August 28, 2003. www.boston.com.
Bonnie Kerness	"America's Abuse of Prisoners Didn't Begin in Iraq—a Personal Reflection" *Watching Justice,* May 24, 2004. www.watchingjustice.org.
Joseph F. McDonough	"Prison Education Programs Cut Rate of Reoffending," *Boston Globe,* July 13, 2004. www.boston.com.
Dorothy E. Roberts	"The Social and Moral Cost of Mass Incarceration in African American Communities," *Stanford Law Review,* April 2004.
Darrell A. Siggers	"Dodging Prison Doors;" *Detroit Free Press,* July 13, 2005.

Leah Thayer	"Hidden Hell: Women in Prison," *Amnesty Magazine*, Fall 2004. www.amnestyusa.org.
Richard D. Vogel	"Silencing the Cells: Mass Incarceration and Legal Repression in U.S. Prisons," *Monthly Review*, May, 2004. www.monthlyreview.org.
Peter Wagner	"Locked Up, Then Counted Out: Prisoners and the Census." *Fortune News*, Winter 2002–2003.
Western Prison Project	"Torture and Abuse in Prison," *Justice Matters*, Summer 2004.
Armstrong Williams	"The Culture of Violence," *Townhall.com*, May 10, 2004. www.townhall.com.

CHAPTER 3

How Should Prisons Operate?

Chapter Preface

In deciding how prisons should be run, debate often centers on what kinds of programs should be offered to inmates. Along with work opportunities and drug treatment programs, prisoner education has many advocates, who say that it helps rehabilitate inmates and cut down on recidivism. Research by the University of California at Los Angeles School of Public Policy for the U.S. Department of Education, Office of Correctional Education, found that "one million dollars spent on correctional education prevents about 600 crimes, while that same money invested in incarceration prevents 350 crimes." According to the 2004 study, "Inmates who participate in education programs are less likely to return to prison. For each re-incarceration prevented by education, states save about $20,000." An especially important aim of prisoner education programs, advocates assert, is increased literacy. According to Stuart Henry, a professor at Wayne State University, "Research has consistently demonstrated that the most effective way to reduce offending, and particularly reoffending, is through education, particularly literacy training and GED [general equivalency diploma]."

Despite widespread support, inmate education programs have been cut in many prisons due to state budget shortfalls. In 2003 the Justice Policy Institute issued the report *Education and Incarceration* showing that not only is incarceration in America's prisons and jails "highly concentrated among men with little schooling, but corrections systems are doing less and less to 'correct' the problem by reducing educational opportunities for the growing number of prisoners." The editors of the Springfield, Missouri, *News Leader* contend that "it is in the state's interest, it is in communities' interest, and it is in citizens' interest to see that inmates can succeed. Budget cuts that make that more difficult will only cost us all much more, in pain and in money."

Even though budget shortfalls are making it more difficult for prisons to offer education to inmates, supporters continue to work for increased educational opportunities for prisoners. Advocates of correctional education endorse new legislation that would increase educational program requirements in prison and provide incentives for participation and success. The Literacy, Education, and Rehabilitation Act (H.R. 3602), referred to the House Committee on the Judiciary on July 28, 2005, proposes to amend the federal criminal code to "award credit toward the service of a sentence to prisoners who participate in designated education, vocation, treatment, assigned work, or other developmental programs."

Whether or not the act will pass remains to be seen. Regardless, supporters of prison education will likely remain steadfast in their belief in the power of education to transform inmates. Authors in the following chapter examine other issues pertaining to how prisons should operate. As budget shortfalls continue in most states, prison officials will have to run their institutions even more efficiently, which may necessitate cutting beneficial programs such as prisoner education.

"[A Vanderbilt University] study found states that utilized private prisons had considerably more success in keeping their total public corrections spending under control than states with no private prisons."

Privately Operated Prisons Are Beneficial

Geoffrey F. Segal

Geoffrey F. Segal is director of privatization and government reform policy at the Reason Foundation and a research fellow at the Davenport Institute at Pepperdine University's School of Public Policy. Segal cites two research studies supporting his claim that states choosing to have some of their prisons run by private companies will save public money. He contends that longer prison sentences and more crowded prisons will result in a bigger market for the private prison industry. Increased privatization of prison systems, he argues, will bring increased savings in operating costs.

As you read, consider the following questions:

1. What percentage of U.S. states host private prisons, as cited by Segal?
2. In the Vanderbilt University study, what amount of savings in public prison operating costs did researchers predict for states introducing competition and privatization?
3. Which U. S. state leads the nation in prison privatization, as reported by the author?

Geoffrey F. Segal, "Private Prisons Save Money, Boost Productivity, Studies Find," www.heartland.com, November 11, 2003. Copyright © 2003 by The Heartland Institute. Reproduced by permission.

In a get-tough-on-crime move nearly a decade ago, Florida passed in 1995 a law requiring all prison inmates to serve at least 85 percent of their sentences. Since then, the amount of time most inmates spend behind bars in the Sunshine State has increased dramatically, putting privatization on the table for Florida policymakers.

Longer sentences mean more crowded prisons and a bigger market for the private prison industry, said Alan Duffee, executive director of the Correctional Privatization Commission that oversees Florida's five private prisons. "That has been an effect of [the 85 percent law]," Duffee said. "We have fewer inmates (going) out than coming in."

According to the Los Angeles, California-based Reason Foundation, new research shows private prisons are "a viable alternative for addressing state budget and cost concerns"— not only in Florida, but across the United States.

Privatization and Competition

Three-fifths of all U.S. states host private prisons; most of them contract with the companies to house prisoners. Studies show privatization can result in savings in the range of 5 to 20 percent. Adding to that body of research, two new studies take a slightly different approach to estimating the cost savings associated with prison privatization.

By measuring an entire department's spending rather than just a particular prison's spending, the studies account for the cost savings that result when public prisons respond to private competition.

In an August 2003 report, two professors at Vanderbilt University analyzed whether the use of private prisons by state correctional departments had any effect on the rate of growth in the operating budgets of state corrections systems. While anecdotal evidence existed in Texas and Arizona, a systematic analysis had never been done.

Using data for 1999–2001, [a Vanderbilt University] study found states that utilized private prisons had considerably more success in keeping their total public corrections spending under control than states with no private prisons.

During the period studied, the daily cost of housing prisoners grew 8.9 percent more slowly in states with private prisons than in states without them.

In 2001, according to the study, states without private prisons spent $445 million a year on average for their corrections systems. The researchers projected the average state in that group could save $20 million a year in public prison operating costs simply by introducing competition and prison privatization. Further savings would be achieved through the actual operation of the private prisons themselves.

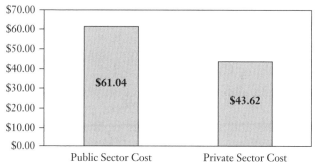

Average Inmate Cost Per Day: A Public/ Private Cost Comparison

Geoffrey F. Segal, "Increased Competition in Department of Corrections Will Lead to Additional Savings," June 17, 2003. www.rppi.org.

Importantly, the Vanderbilt University researchers also found that turning over to the private sector even the smallest of prison populations results in big savings. States with less than 5 percent of their prison population in private facilities experienced a 12.5 percent increase in expenditures over the period studied, versus an 18.9 percent increase for states without private prisons. States that had turned over larger shares of their prison populations to private management experienced even greater savings: Expenditure growth was just 5.9 percent for this group over the period studied.

In a second study, researchers at the Rio Grande Foundation in New Mexico compared per-prisoner department of corrections budgets across 46 states. The study uses the percentage of prisoners under private management as its measurement of the extent of privatization in each state. The author controlled for factors that affect a corrections department's per-prisoner cost: market wage for prison employees, prison crowding, and labor conditions, for example.

Holding other factors constant, the Rio Grande study found states with 5 percent of their prison population in private prisons spent about $4,804 less per prisoner in 2001 than states without any privatization.

As the extent of privatization increases, so do savings. New Mexico, for example, has 45 percent of its prison population under private management; it spent $9,660 less per prisoner in 2001 than did counterpart states with no privatization. New Mexico has gone farther down the prison privatization road than any other state—saving $51 million in 2001 alone, according to the Rio Grande study.

A Compelling Case

While the Vanderbilt study looked at privatization's effect on the growth of prison expenditures over time, the Rio Grande study was more a snapshot of how privatization affected corrections spending in 2001. While the two studies didn't measure the same things, the results are complementary and make a compelling case.

States that utilize competition and privatization for corrections save money. The more a state competes and privatizes, the more money it saves.

The experience of competition and privatization has been well documented across a broad range of services. These two studies represent another feather in the cap for privatization, and a continued solution for the state of Florida.

"The U.S. certainly does not need companies with a vested financial interest in further growth influencing our justice policies."

Privately Operated Prisons Are Not Beneficial

Jenni Gainsborough

Jenni Gainsborough is director of the Washington office of Penal Reform International. In this viewpoint she lists numerous management failures of the Corrections Corporation of America, a leader in prison privatization. Gainsborough cites a 2003 report that documents numerous failures in prison management in privately run prisons. She contends that private prison corporations can promise a cheaper alternative to government only by cutting wages, training, and jobs for correctional officers, which has led to increased violence and escapes among prisoners.

As you read, consider the following questions:

1. What are some of the for-profit prison management failures the author cites?
2. What is the position of prison guard unions with regard to privatization of prisons, according to Gainsborough?
3. What does the author argue is the most troubling impact of for-profit companies on justice policy?

For-profit prison companies like CCA [Corrections Corporation of America] have always presented themselves as both cheaper and better than the traditional publicly owned prisons, staffed by state employees. However, from the mayhem and murders at the prison in Youngstown, Ohio, which eventually led to the company paying $1.6 million to prisoners to settle a lawsuit, to a series of wrongful death civil suits, and numerous disturbances and escapes, the authors [of the 2003 Grass Roots Leadership report] document in detail a staggering range of failures of prison management.

- failure to provide adequate medical care to prisoners;
- failure to control violence in its prisons;
- substandard conditions that have resulted in prisoner protests and uprisings;
- criminal activity on the part of some CCA employees, including the sale of illegal drugs to prisoners; and
- escapes, which in the case of at least two facilities include inadvertent releases of prisoners who were supposed to remain in custody.

Many of the company's problems are blamed on its labor policies. Because prisons are very labor intensive institutions, the only way a company like CCA can sell itself to government as a cheaper option than public prisons while still making a profit, is by using as few staff as possible, paying them as little as possible, and not spending much on training.

Low Wages, High Turnover

From the beginning, CCA has sought to depress its labor costs by keeping wages low and by denying its employees traditional (defined-benefit) pension plans. One predictable result of these policies had been understaffing and high rates of turnover at some of its facilities. For example, annual turnover rates at several CCA facilities in Tennessee have been more than 60 percent. Another, equally predictable, has been the opposition of public service unions to the spread of prison privatization. Criminal justice reformers, trying to reduce the use of incarceration in the U.S., don't normally find themselves allying with prison guard unions but in this fight they are all on the same side.

Despite this opposition, CCA has been quite successful in recent years in influencing the public debate and winning the support of legislators. Of course, it is not hard to win legislators when you back up your arguments with hard cash. The company spends hundreds of thousands of dollars during each state election cycle to try to gain access and build support for its projects. At the federal level, CCA has given more than $100,000 in soft money to the Republican Party since 1997 as well as political action committee contributions to individual members of key Congressional committees.

Private Prisons Put Public Safety at Risk

Since 2000, a wide range of private-prison studies have concluded that state governments are shifting course and moving away from for-profit vendors by not soliciting new contracts or are rescinding others. The researchers have determined that the private facilities produce no tangible savings to taxpayers. If anything, those facilities are chock full of hidden costs.

In addition, employees are generally underpaid and receive few benefits, leading to high turnover rates and inexperienced, untrained replacements. Their safety—and the public's—is at higher risk.

"Supporting Private Prisons: How Far Will the Feds Go?" AFSCME Corrections United, Fall 2002. www.afscme.org.

The presence of J. Michael Quinlan, the former head of the Federal Bureau of Prisons, among CCA's senior executives has surely helped the growth in its contracts with the Federal Bureau of Prisons, and the expectation of further expansion as more prisons for immigrants are planned. In its home state of Tennessee, CCA has enjoyed close relationships with many powerful public figures, including governors. And the for-profit prison companies have their own trade association lobbying for them on Capitol Hill—the Association of Private Correctional and Treatment Organizations (APCTO).

While all of that might be dismissed as no more than the typical business-building efforts of any company looking to make a profit for its shareholders, there are other more troubling aspects to CCA's behavior.

Dubious Research

One has been its use of research from dubious sources to push its claims of superiority and cost-savings for the private sector. Much of it is produced by researchers who are either funded by the industry or are ideologically predisposed in favor of privatization. For example, Charles Thomas, director of the supposedly neutral Private Prison Project of the University of Florida who was widely quoted as an expert on prison privatization throughout the 90s, served on the board of CCA and received several millions of dollars in consulting fees from them.

More recently, a study published in the *Harvard Law Review* was touted as an independent academic study of privatization. None of its boosters, however, mentioned that the author, in addition to being a graduate student at Harvard, is associated with the Reason Public Policy Institute, a division of the Reason Foundation whose purpose is to promote the privatization of public services.

Perhaps most controversial is CCA's close ties to the American Legislative Exchange Council (ALEC). ALEC is a powerful force in the promotion of the conservative policy agenda among state legislators. One of its major functions is writing model bills that advance conservative principles and working with its members to have these bills introduced. CCA has been a corporate member and a major contributor to ALEC and a member of its Criminal Justice Task Force. CCA executives have co-chaired the Task Force over many years. As a result of the model bills developed by the Task Force, ALEC claims credit for the widespread adoption of Truth in Sentencing and Three Strikes/Habitual Offender legislation. Through its support of ALEC, CCA is helping to create greater demand for its services as a result of changes in state policies that keep more people behind bars for longer periods.

Although this aspect of its work is not given a major emphasis in the report, it surely represents the most troubling impact of for-profit prison companies. With more than two million people behind bars and the highest rate of incarceration in the world, the U.S. certainly does not need companies with a vested financial interest in further growth influencing our justice policies.

"It makes no sense to deprive inmates of work, especially since they owe serious debts to others, including victims, 'outmates' and taxpayers."

Prison Labor Benefits Inmates

Morgan Reynolds

Morgan Reynolds is chief economist for the U.S. Department of Labor, on leave as director of the Criminal Justice Center at the National Center for Policy Analysis. In this viewpoint Reynolds argues that the labor of America's prisoners can be part of the solution to a projected shortfall of available American workers. Reynolds contends that U.S. jails and prisons provide too few productive work opportunities to help prisoners acquire good work habits. He considers unemployment in prison to be an immoral abuse of prisoners.

As you read, consider the following questions:

1. What does Reynolds say is the best predictor of post-release success for former prisoners?
2. What criticisms does Reynolds have of federal prison industries?
3. What conditions does the author say are required for bringing prison work-force performance up to par with its free-world counterpart?

P risons have broken the back of our 35-year crime wave. It's about that simple.

Our economy will create some 19 million jobs by 2006 according to government studies, but the projected number of people available to work is supposed to only increase by 15 million. That's a shortfall of 4 million workers in an economy with only 1.5 million currently unemployed for 15 weeks or longer.

Part of the answer to this problem is to put prisoners to work. It makes no sense to deprive inmates of work, especially since they owe serious debts to others, including victims, "outmates" and taxpayers. Yet our jails and prisons do little or nothing to provide productive work opportunities. Once upon a time, the common wisdom was that prisoners should work but now it's mostly banned. Opponents claim that it's unfair competition.

The result is that jails and prisons—our "correctional" institutions—reek of idleness and fail to correct. Only 80,000 inmates out of 1.8 million people behind bars today—fewer than one in twenty—have jobs producing something useful for the outside world, whether for the private market or government agencies (classic product: license plates). Fewer than 5,000 work for capitalist enterprises, while the rest work for socialist prison industry.

News item: Socialism does not work, inside or outside prison. Capitalism works. This fact is only disputed on college campuses, homes for aging radicals. Prison-made goods may have a reputation for inferior design, workmanship and reliability but that's because it's produced under socialism, which produces junk. Prison industries face no competitive pressure on quality and price, deliberately aim at inefficiency in order to give inmates something to do, pay zero or trivial wages (allowing the luxury of overstaffing and inefficiency), and fail to recruit qualified personnel from private industry to administer production programs. So we get indolence, apathy, boredom and no skills or work habits, a formula that fails to steer inmates into productive roles in society.

The answer is clear: unleash entrepreneurs to put prisoners' idle time to productive use in exchange for real wages. Only business can succeed in business. Make it as real world as possible. Prison administrators should act like "Manpower Inc." or "Kelly Services" [employment agencies] and try to rent their labor forces for the highest and best terms available. The historical evidence shows that when reasonable incentives, humane working conditions and prison labor are combined with the profit motive, the performance of a prison work force is at least as good as its free-world counterpart. A recent Deloitte Touche study found that in four out of four cases productivity was as good or higher with prison labor forces.

Study after study shows that inmate work is the best predictor of postrelease success. And it's not so much learning

---

The Advantages of Prison Labor

FPI [Federal Prison Industries] is, first and foremost, a correctional program. The whole impetus behind Federal Prison Industries is not about business, but instead, about inmate release preparation . . . helping offenders acquire the skills necessary to successfully make that transition from prison to law-abiding, contributing members of society. The production of items and provision of services are merely by-products of those efforts.

Other program benefits. . . .

• *to society*—Rigorous research demonstrates that participation in prison industries and vocational training programs has a positive effect on post-release employment and recidivism for up to 12 years following release. . . .

• *to the courts, crime victims, and inmate families*—In FY [fiscal year] 2004, inmates who worked in FPI factories contributed over $3 million of their earnings toward meeting their financial obligations, e.g., court-ordered fines, child support, and/or restitution. . . .

• The program teaches inmates pro-social values including the value of work, responsibility, and the need to respect and work with others. . . .

• *to private sector businesses*—During FY 2004, FPI purchased approximately $514.6 million in raw materials, supplies, equipment, and services from private sector businesses. . . .

• *to the Bureau of Prisons*—FPI contributes significantly to the safety and security of federal correctional facilities by keeping inmates constructively occupied.

UNICOR Federal Prison Industries. www.unicor.gov, November 22, 2005.

---

technical skills that matters but acquiring good work habits like reliability, neatness, willingness to learn, and friendliness and cooperation on the job. A job behind bars is the only regular job most inmates have ever had and relationships with supervisors are the most rehabilitative human connection that prisoners have.

But isn't prison work "slave labor" and an abuse of human rights? No. Given an opportunity for humane and productive work at a federal minimum wage, prisoners line up for it, compete for it, and try their best at it.

Work is not the abuse. On the contrary, the abuse is adding compulsory unemployment on top of deprivation of liberty. As Australian criminologist John Braithwaite said, prisoners "have a right to work and make a productive contribution to the nation equal to that of any citizen. Their punishment is confinement, not enforced idleness." It is immoral to deny work permanently to prisoners.

"In states like Wisconsin and California, prisoners work in jailhouse factories for third-world wages."

Prison Labor Exploits Inmates

Brandi Kishner

The goal of prison labor is not to rehabilitate prisoners, claims Brandi Kishner in the following viewpoint. In fact, she argues, most American prisons exploit inmates by placing profits before rehabilitation. Rather than invest in training that might help prisoners find jobs outside of prison, prisons put inmates to work using skills that they already have, Kishner asserts. Indeed, she maintains, many are overqualified for the jobs they perform in prison. Kishner writes for *People's Weekly World*, a socialist newspaper.

As you read, consider the following questions:

1. According to Kishner, in what unique ways does Vermont use prison labor?
2. In the author's view, what can happen in communities where prison labor takes jobs away from the working class?
3. Why do capitalist ventures minimize investment in training, in the author's opinion?

Brandi Kishner "Prison Labor Needs Reforms," *People's Weekly World*," November 23, 2003. Reproduced by permission.

The practice of prison labor is almost as old as the ages. In fact, many forms of ancient slavery lie in the use of conquered people for work. Currently, the idea and practice of prison labor is as diverse as it is controversial. Arguments for and against it are often based on broad assumptions about how and why prison labor is used.

For example, in Vermont a new system of prison labor is currently employed that doesn't fit the standard chain-gang or license plate mold. Prisoners at one small county jail are free to work in their community at fair market wages, with modest deductions for their room and board and other reasonable costs, such as child support. Prisoners do not work inside the prison but work at normal jobs; they wear normal clothes, not jailhouse blues; they maintain normal community ties and are not subjected to any form of dehumanization or disrespect as a result of their imprisonment, and they are free to work real jobs by which they can maintain themselves and their families after their term of incarceration. In this one Vermont jail, prisoners are really reintegrated into society; rehabilitation is the underlying motivation, not a by-product of profits.

The Reality of Prison Labor

But this lone Vermont phenomenon is in direct contrast to the rest of the nation's prison-industrial complex. In states like Wisconsin and California, prisoners work in jailhouse factories for third-world wages. Furthermore, rather than being equal competitors to their unincarcerated counterparts, they are actually state-subsidized monopolistic forces, taking jobs away from hard-working Americans in industries like manufacturing and telemarketing.

State and federal agencies claim that prison industry is rehabilitating convicts with job training, encouraging a work ethic and discipline, giving prisoners the skills that will allow them to be successful outside of prison. However, most prison industry is in the manufacturing sector, the very industry that is already on the decline in the American job market.

Far from being trained for life outside of prison, in California prisoners are surveyed for over 50 skills that they already possess upon arrival and are generally put to work doing tasks that they already know how to do. In South Carolina, at Evans Correctional Facility, over 250 jailhouse workers are working for an IBM supplier and "many inmate workers are over-qualified for the jobs they hold," according to Bert Christy, a plant manager at the site, quoted in a February 1999 article in *Perspective Magazine*.

Anderson. © 1996 by Kirk Anderson. Reproduced by permission.

There are also numerous cases of convicts working as telemarketers taking credit card information, although most telemarketing firms would not hire ex-convicts, even if they were already trained. Indeed prison labor is taking jobs away from the working class in many communities, which in turn encourages higher rates of incarceration in those very same communities.

Rather than offering substantial job training to encourage market growth, prisons are being used to nail the coffin door closed on industries that are already reeling from the effects of globalization. Furthermore, when short-term profits are the driving force for prison labor, it is virtually guaranteed that convicts are not being trained for a wide range of jobs that they might actually get in the non-prison world. This is because training is an investment which capitalist ventures desire to minimize. It's not profitable in the short term to train large numbers of convicts on a variety of jobs; rather they will be kept to what is most efficient.

Until our society stops manufacturing criminals, it is best if those who are jailed are not idle, so in the meantime their activities should be individually focused on their talents and potentials, to provide each person with the best path toward a fulfilling and productive life. And that should not be confused with expedient profits. Job training is a good so long as it is not just mindless activity.

"Inmates must accept some financial responsibility in the reimbursement of their housing, thus taking the first step in becoming productive members of their community."

Prisoners Should Be Charged for Prison Costs

Michelle M. Sanborn

Michelle M. Sanborn is jail administrator at the Macomb County Sheriff's Office in Mt. Clemens, Michigan. In this viewpoint Sanborn defends the twenty-year old state legislation allowing collection of expenses from Michigan inmates. Such programs work to encourage financial responsibility on the inmates' part, she argues, and provide a cost savings to taxpayers. The author contends that persons convicted of criminal wrongdoing should not further victimize the public by burdening it with the high costs of incarceration.

As you read, consider the following questions:

1. How successful have the pay-to-stay programs been in Michigan, according to Sanborn?
2. In the author's opinion, why are co-payments required for prison medical care?
3. How will funds collected from inmates benefit the community, in Sanborn's view?

Michelle M. Sanborn, "The Pay-to-Stay Debate: Inmates Must Take Financial Responsibility," *Corrections Today*, vol. 65, August 2003, p. 22. Copyright © 2003 by the American Correctional Association. Reproduced by permission.

In responding to the continuing upward spiral of financing jail operations, William Hacket, former Macomb County, Mich., sheriff, and the Macomb County Board of Commissioners in 1985 implemented one of the nation's first inmate pay-to-stay programs. The program was initiated pursuant to the provisions of the 1984 Prisoner Reimbursement to the County Act. The Michigan state law allows counties to collect fees for services and seek reimbursement from sentenced inmates for room and board expenses.

Nearly 20 years ago, when the legislation passed, the thought was that successful collection of expenses from inmates was impossible. The law was viewed as conceptually attractive by taxpayers but realistically, an attempt in futility. There was some public contention that the legislation created a debtor's prison. Their feeling was that convicted offenders should not be forced to pay for their stay in addition to serving time. This is wrong.

Inmates continue to be a financial burden to society. The local jails are viewed as another county service that drains taxpayer dollars—dollars that could be better spent in the community for libraries, parks, schools and the like. Funding jail operations and new jail construction is never socially attractive and is typically avoided at all costs. The above allocations are much more palatable when a revenue source exists. This is especially appealing when the source is from inmates who reimburse the county for their stay and services provided to them while incarcerated.

By assessing fees and seeking reimbursement, the costs recovered, if not returned to the county, might be used to benefit inmates by purchasing books, clothing, hygiene items, security equipment for visiting, etc., which are otherwise budgeted items.

Most pay-to-stay programs follow a sliding scale to assess room and board fees and charge nominal amounts for services and consumables. This effort recoups only a portion of the expense in housing. No one is turning a profit. Also, indirect benefits of having a pay-to-stay program are realized as cost savings, more effective use of resources and an opportunity to improve safety and security of the facility.

The charging of co-pays for medical expenses further reduces frivolous requests for services by inmates wishing to pass idle time, get out of their unit or simply visit with the nurse. Medical personnel can more effectively assess and treat the individuals who are truly in need of those services. Less money is spent for over-the-counter wraps, aids, ointments and medication given to inmates. Facility security benefits with a direct reduction of inmate movement, allowing for the reallocation of manpower. Also, charging for other items, such as damaged property toiletries, haircuts etc., allows for additional cost savings as inmates are less inclined to abuse, misuse and lose these things when there is an associated cost.

Reducing the Cost of Incarceration

Most states have laws allowing local jails to impose some fees on inmates. The fees can be for room and board, telephone usage, and haircuts but most typically, medical care. Savings would be realized by reducing the overutilization of services.

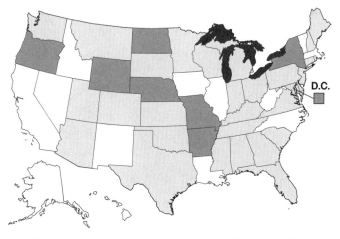

State prison inmate medical co-pays, October 2003

No medical co-pay plan $2–$5 fee per medical visit   No data

Note: Colorado uses a tiered system but is reviewing a co-pay plan.

National Institute of Corrections. www.detnews.com.

Typically, the cost of operating our jails represents a major portion of county budgets and a substantial amount of liability. Taxpayers historically have had to bear the expense for offender apprehension, prosecution and detention. They are also burdened with providing food, clothing, housing, health care and other cost-related expenses to offenders housed and/or convicted of criminal wrongdoing. One might ask why law-abiding citizens should be burdened with the cost of incarceration when they never use that service or why taxpayers should be further victimized by supporting inmates who have the wherewithal to pay.

In debating whether it is right or wrong to charge inmates, consider the fact that we have a financial obligation to our respective communities. Part of our responsibility as corrections professionals is to provide programs in the hope of teaching some basic life skills and providing treatment services where needed to stop the vicious cycle of recidivism. Institutionalizing offenders is sometimes not enough of a deterrent. Inmates must accept some financial responsibility in the reimbursement of their housing, thus taking the first step in becoming productive members of their community.

"To charge $5 a day to the person committed to a State/County correctional facility only furthers desperation and oppression in the lives of that person and their family. It makes a bad circumstance even worse."

Prisoners Should Not Be Charged for Prison Costs

Phebe Eckfeldt

Phebe Eckfeldt is a reporter for *Workers World* newspaper. In this viewpoint Eckfeldt challenges a Massachusetts attempt to balance the budget by charging state prisoners $5 a day toward the cost of their incarceration. The author reports that prisoners at the super maximum security prison who protested the fee risked repercussions from prison authorities. One inmate-organizer was placed in segregation and denied library and work privileges, she claims. Eckfeldt suggests that requiring inmates to pay prison costs dooms society's most desperate members.

As you read, consider the following questions:

1. According to the author, why did the state of Massachusetts decide to charge prisoners for the costs of incarceration?
2. What other costs, according to Eckfeldt, do prisoners have to pay during their stay in a Massachusetts prison?
3. What percentage of earnings will released prisoners be forced to pay for any accrued debt during their prison time, according to the author?

Phebe Eckfeldt, "Should Prisoner's Pay Rent? They Say No!," *Worker's World*, August 29, 2002. Copyright © 2002 by *Worker's World*. Reproduced by permission.

An attempt by the state of Massachusetts to balance the budget on the backs of the poorest of the poor—prisoners—is meeting heroic resistance from prisoners themselves.

This spring [2002] the state came up $2 billion short in tax revenues and began slashing social-service programs. In a desperate attempt to raise funds, the government attached language to the appropriation line item for the operation of the Office of the Commissioner of Public Safety that requires prisoners to pay $5 a day towards the cost of their incarceration.

House Budget Line 8000-0000, as it is called, would give the state the power to take that money out of prisoner's canteen funds or their pay, if they have jobs.

Prisoners are already forced to buy all their personal items such as soap, deodorant, toothpaste, toilet paper, clothing, footwear and medications from the prison-run canteen.

In addition, the state would force released inmates to pay up to 25 percent of their earnings from any job on the outside in order to pay back the accrued debt. It is estimated that a prisoner released after serving five years would owe more than $9,000.

When in the spring the warden at the Bristol County House of Corrections arbitrarily decided to impose this $5-a-day fee before the law was passed, prisoners rebelled for two days. On Aug. 7 a lawsuit was filed against this fee on the prisoners' behalf.

Item 8000-0000 has passed the State House of Representatives and is now before the Senate. Proponents say that it would generate $1.1 million in revenue from prisoners and their families.

Prisoner Leads Protest

Nathaniel Atkins is an inmate serving a double life sentence at the Souza-Baranowski Correctional Center (SBCC) in Shirley, Mass. At great personal risk, Atkins, along with other inmates, wrote a sample letter protesting this attack. Prisoners were asked to get family members, friends and other supporters to send this letter to their senators in protest.

The letter says the budget rider "is designed to guarantee that poor people who become incarcerated will be consigned to degrading sub-poverty status for the rest of their lives. A financial slavery that will extend for many years after their release from prison.

"To charge $5 a day to the person committed to a State/County correctional facility only furthers desperation and oppression in the lives of that person and their family. It makes a bad circumstance even worse. A huge majority of the incarcerated are at a poverty level to begin with and they have family to support.

High Rent Prison

After more than two years behind bars, recovering narcotics addict Kathleen White figured she'd paid her debt to society.

She was wrong. . . .

White received an unexpected correspondence from the state Department of Administrative Services: an itemized bill for $67,165, which the Department of Correction says was the cost of her incarcerations. . . .

According to the itemized bill White received from Connecticut, she owes $25,970 for an 8½-month incarceration in 1999, $17,778 for two stints behind bars totaling about six months in 2002, and $23,424 for an eight-month sentence that ended in June 2004.

During that time, White maintains she was incarcerated in barely livable conditions at the York Correctional Institution in East Lyme, working for pennies an hour, and said she was forced to buy necessities such as shampoo and toothpaste at vastly inflated prices at the prison store. . . .

"How am I ever going to get on my feet if they're going to take over everything I get?" she asked.

"State Wants Former Inmate to Pay Cost of Incarceration." New Haven, CT, www.nhregister.com.

Allowing this $5 a day to accrue and then the bill managed by probation/parole to be paid after the person wraps up a sentence is legalizing extortion. It is also a motive for someone NOT to seek legitimate employment upon completion of his sentence."

At SBCC jobs are available for only around 20 percent of the prisoners and the average pay is $1.50 per day. Working six days per week, this translates into $9.00 per week.

To add insult to injury, Line Item 8000-0000 also states

that if a prisoner is found responsible for injuring a guard and the guard needs workers' compensation or has medical bills as a result, the prisoner will be responsible for those costs. Many observers consider these new rules an expansion of racism, as in Massachusetts African American men make up 40 percent of the prison population but only 5.4 percent of the state population.

SBCC is a super-max, high-tech prison. Prisoners are kept in their cells 20 hours a day. Contact among prisoners in a cellblock is only possible for very short periods during gym and yard time and 20 minutes during meals.

Despite this isolation, Atkins and fellow prisoner activists were able to flood the entire prison with this letter, reaching all 16 cell blocks with 64 men per block. This underscores the tremendous respect Atkins has earned over the years as a political activist.

Prison Authorities Frame Atkins

To stop his organizing and remove him from the general population, the Department of Corrections decided to frame up Atkins on bogus charges. A prison informant told authorities Atkins said he would take the superintendent hostage if the bill passed.

Atkins was thrown into the segregation unit where a prisoner is confined to a 7-foot by 10-foot cell 23 hours a day for five days a week and 24 hours a day for the other two. Abuse by guards is random, arbitrary and frequent. No televisions or radios are allowed, only Walkmans, a Bible or Koran and first-class mail. Human contact is irregular and infrequent and only with staff.

Atkins remained in segregation for 43 days. But he refused to be intimidated and managed to continue to educate other prisoners in the segregation unit on this issue.

Atkins' supporters were able to secure legal assistance for his disciplinary board hearing and in writing his subsequent appeal. Recently the Department of Corrections ruled Atkins guilty on two charges, including threatening the warden. His punishment is the loss of six weeks of library time and no work anywhere for six months. This translates into total loss of income.

Atkins told *Workers World*, "People cannot concern themselves with individual repercussions because that isn't what it's all about—the individual. It's about the collective, the good for the whole. Someone has to step forward to fight the good fight. We all know a standing stream will become stale and putrid so to keep it healthy you must agitate, agitate and agitate."

"What Prison Fellowship provides in Inner-Change Freedom Initiative is not only skills, but hearts that have been transformed."

Faith-Based Programs Benefit Prisoners

Melissa Rogers

Melissa Rogers is visiting professor of religion and public policy at Wake Forest University Divinity School. In this viewpoint Rogers contends that the InnerChange Freedom Initiative, a Christian program providing prerelease services to prisoners, is a faith-based solution that works. Rogers argues that the voluntary program does not require Christian faith as a prerequisite for participation or graduation, and protects the religious nature of the service providers as well as the religious freedom of participants and nonparticipants. The program, she argues, has been effective in breaking the cycle of recidivism.

As you read, consider the following question:
1. Which prisoners are eligible to join the faith-based program, according to Rogers?
2. In the author's view, what benefits do participants in the InnerChange Initiative receive?
3. Are there similar programs available to other faith groups, according to the author?

Melissa Rogers, "The Story of Inner Change Freedom Initiative," *Liberty Online: A Magazine of Religious Freedom*, September/October 2003. Copyright © 2003 by *Liberty Online*, www.libertymagazine.com. Reproduced by permission.

InnerChange Freedom Initiative is based on a set of values that are the polar opposite of the values that predominate among prisoners and in the culture that breeds them. We believe that if a prisoner is going to get out of prison and contribute to society, he needs to adopt a whole new way of looking at the world and at others. That is, we believe he will need to be transformed from the inside. Without God in the picture, a prisoner is much more likely to slip back into old ways. With God, all things are possible.

The core values of InnerChange Freedom Initiative are Integrity/Truth, Fellowship, Affirmation, Responsibility/ Restoration, and Productivity.

Core Values

Integrity/Truth. It should come as no surprise that honesty is not a value common among criminals. InnerChange Freedom Initiative participants are taught the value of truth and truth telling. Prisoners are encouraged to see how personal integrity will promote their success whether in prison or out. The core value of truth is also an assertion that there is absolute truth that can be known through natural law and biblical revelation.

Fellowship. Fellowship is the value that builds community in the program. The unity prisoners feel in the program is based on their shared commitment to submit their lives to God. Prisoners are taught that just as God loves them unconditionally, they need to reflect the same kind of love to those around them. To help in this, each participant has a mentor who stays with him through the transition from prison to life on the outside. Fellowship continues when prisoners leave and choose to join local churches where they can continue to be affirmed and held accountable.

Affirmation. This is a value both in InnerChange Freedom Initiative and in more therapeutic models of prisoner rehabilitation. Many inmates have never experienced affirmation and do not know what it means to be valued. Others have been affirmed in wrong attitudes, false values, and criminal behavior. In IFI we believe affirmation flows from trust in a loving God and is an affirmation for good.

Responsibility/Restoration. InnerChange Freedom Initiative places a heavy emphasis on taking responsibility for choices. Participants take responsibility for their actions by initiating acts of healing and reconciliation with those they have victimized, alienated, and hurt. For example, participants are encouraged to write to their victims, admitting their crimes and asking forgiveness. This sets not only the prisoner but often the victim free, and we have seen remarkable friendships develop between prisoners and their victims. In this way prisoners are restored to their Creator, their families, and their communities.

Productivity. The Bible has a high view of productivity and work; most inmates have a very low view of productivity and work. InnerChange Freedom Initiative defines productivity as the wise use of time in accordance with God's principles for life. Participants learn to set goals and priorities and to balance work, worship, and rest. IFI teaches job skills, but we know that those skills will come to nothing without the value of productivity driving behavior.

A Voluntary Program

From the very beginning InnerChange Freedom Initiative has been voluntary. The only states that have InnerChange Freedom Initiative programs are states that have invited it into their prisons.

Similarly, all participation in InnerChange Freedom Initiative is voluntary. Prisoners apply for the program and are fully briefed on the values-based, Christian character of the program. They also know that Christian faith, or faith of any kind, is not a prerequisite for participation or graduation. . . .

We make it clear that InnerChange Freedom Initiative is not a path to an easier life in prison. On the contrary, IFI places more structure and more demands on the prisoners. During a typical day at InnerChange Freedom Initiative, prisoners wake up at 5:00 A.M. and eat breakfast at 5:30. Morning devotions begin at 6:00 a.m., followed by school, work, or daily living skills classes and leadership training. Life skills include literacy, how to find a job, and financial management. These classes run from 7:00 in the morning to 3:00 in the afternoon. After dinner there are more classes, a study period, and lights out. Every day is full and highly structured.

And InnerChange Freedom Initiative prisoners do not watch television. Overall, it is far easier to stay in the general prison population and avoid the extra programs, responsibilities, and discipline that are central to InnerChange Freedom Initiative. Participants work hard for what they achieve.

Reforming Prisoners—Body and Soul

While the state exerts external coercive force to punish crime, faith-based community groups are able to address the internal spiritual issues at the core of evil activity. Charles Colson's Prison Fellowship Ministries is just one example of many organizations that focus on effectively ministering to prisoners. Because these community groups are private and not subject to the restrictions binding government agencies, they are able to engage prisoners on a personal and spiritual level, focusing on the needs of the whole human person, body and soul. . . .

The activities of faith-based organizations like Prison Fellowship Ministries are necessary complements to the state's enforcement of criminal punishments. In order to effectively address the future of those who have committed crimes, government officials and politicians must continue to increase their recognition of the critical role these private institutions play in the reform of criminals and the contribution to a healthy and vibrant society.

Jordan J. Ballor, "Magistrates and Ministers," Action Institute for the Study of Religion and Liberty, August 11, 2004. www.acton.org.

The InnerChange Freedom Initiative programs that operate in Texas, Kansas, Minnesota, and Iowa in no way violate the establishment clause of the First Amendment to the Constitution. In fact, the Federal Welfare Reform Law of 1996, signed by President Bill Clinton, allows a state to include religious organizations as social service providers. Congress enacted and President Clinton signed a Charitable Choice provision to encourage states to include overtly religious organizations in the delivery of publicly funded social services. The law protects the religious nature and character of service providers and the religious freedom of participants and nonparticipants. And federal civil rights statutes permit faith-based service providers such as InnerChange Freedom Initiative to hire only staff whose personal beliefs correspond with those of the organization.

Such state-funded religious programming is nothing new in the United States. Most prisons have chaplains from a variety of faith traditions who are employees of the state. In the case of InnerChange Freedom Initiative, no state funds are going to religious programming. IFI uses state monies solely for secular expenses. Prisoners are housed, fed, and taught job and life skills with state funds. The expense of the religious programming is paid for by private donations. InnerChange Freedom Initiative staff members are Prison Fellowship employees, not state employees, and the program relies heavily on volunteers who come from a wide variety of Christian denominations including mainline Presbyterians, Catholics, Southern Baptists, Episcopalians, and United Methodists.

Since its inception in 1997 InnerChange Freedom Initiative has served bank robbers, embezzlers, members of drug cartels, and murderers. Many, such as Michael Potts, were repeat offenders caught in a cycle of recidivism. And InnerChange Freedom Initiative has been effective in breaking that cycle in the lives of men like Michael and men like Victor Sanchez, a former "kingpin drug seller." After Michael completed his prison term and IFI, he started a successful remodeling business. Then he went back to prison as an IFI volunteer. He has been mentoring Victor, who recently left prison and now works for Michael. "IFI really prepared me through training to work on the outside," says Michael. "They put me on the path I needed to be on when I got out." That, in a nutshell, is what InnerChange Freedom Initiative is all about.

A Broken System

The correctional system in America is broken. We have 2 million people in prison, 630,000 getting out this year [2003]. Of those getting out, 60 to 70 percent will be back within two years. If new offenders are entering at a constant rate at the same time, we had better build prisons at a record rate or find a solution to recidivism that works. InnerChange Freedom Initiative has that solution—a faith-based solution.

InnerChange Freedom Initiative has proven to dramatically reduce reincarceration rates among inmates. In February

2003 the Criminal Justice Policy Council in Texas released an evaluation of the Texas program with minimum-security prisoners. The report found that of the inmates who completed the Texas InnerChange Freedom Initiative program, only 8 percent returned to prison within two years, compared with a 22 percent return rate for a comparable group of inmates who were eligible for the program but did not participate and a 42 percent return rate for Texas prisons overall. This is revolutionary progress, and it is good news for America.

What we need in our correctional system is an opportunity for hearts to be transformed, not simply for people to get some job skills. What Prison Fellowship provides in InnerChange Freedom Initiative is not only skills, but hearts that have been transformed through the love of God and the power of the gospel of Jesus Christ. And this is of great benefit to prisoners, their families, their victims, their communities, and, ultimately, our whole society.

> "[Prison Fellowship Ministries] can receive state funds because InnerChange members enroll voluntarily, though it's hard to see the program as entirely voluntary when lifestyle and parole benefits serve as both carrot and stick."

Faith-Based Programs Discriminate Against Prisoners

Samantha M. Shapiro

Samantha M. Shapiro is a writer based in New York City. In this viewpoint Shapiro reports on her visit to the Ellsworth, Kansas, medium security prison. She investigated the Inner-Change Freedom Initiative's 104 bed wing, a part of the Prison Fellowship Ministries' 24-hour immersion program. Shapiro's conversations with prisoners and staff revealed the special privileges granted to participants who join the voluntary Christian program. She claims that many prisoners join the program simply to get out of their cell blocks and enjoy perks, such as free pizza and increased work-release opportunities. Meanwhile, Shapiro maintains, other inmates are denied these advantages, and those wishing to participate in non-Christian religious practices are provided less occasion to do so.

As you read, consider the following questions:

1. According to Shapiro, which prisoners are eligible to join the faith-based program?
2. Are equivalent secular rehabilitation programs an available option to non-Christian prisoners, according to the author?

Samantha M. Shapiro, "Jails for Jesus," *Mother Jones*, November 2003. Copyright © 2003 by the Foundation for National Progress. Reproduced by permission.

P astor Don Raymond isn't trained in corrections and is not employed by the government, but he runs a new 140-person wing of the Ellsworth, Kansas, medium-security prison that draws inmates from throughout the state system. . . .

Raymond's wing, the faith-based InnerChange Freedom Initiative, is identical to the rest of the prison but feels like an entirely different place, an excessively well-lit church basement perhaps. Inmates have arranged their desks, stacked with Bibles and workbooks, in a tidy circle. One rushes to pull a chair out for me; others reach out for a double-handed shake or a shoulder clap poised to morph into a full-body hug. These inmates see plenty of women; Raymond keeps a steady flow of church volunteers, mentors, and teachers circulating throughout the wing. They don't behave toxicly, because the InnerChange staff doesn't treat them like they are murderers or rapists, even though some are. . . .

Aided by friends in high places—such as the White House—legislators in Kansas, Iowa, Texas, and Minnesota have, in the last six years, turned over portions of their prisons, and corrections budgets, to the politically powerful evangelical Christian group, Prison Fellowship Ministries, which pays Raymond's salary. The largest prison ministry in the world, PFM sends more than 50,000 volunteers into prisons in every state with the goal of "declaring the good news of Jesus Christ to those impacted by crime." The Ministries' "Angel Tree" program has presented more than 4 million children of inmates with Christmas presents and evangelistic materials. The goal is clear. As Mark Earley, who was attorney general of Virginia before becoming president of PFM in 2002, writes on its website, "I believe God is going to raise up the next generation of leaders for His Church from men and women now behind bars, and from their children."

In 1997, as part of a larger effort to increase funding for faith-based services in Texas, then-Governor George W. Bush gave PFM the chance to do more than just visit prisons; he allowed it to run a 24-hour "immersion" program in collaboration with the Department of Corrections. Three other states have since followed suit, and PFM plans to be in five more states by 2005. . . .

A Radical Change

In Kansas, most inmates two years away from possible parole are eligible to join InnerChange. Inmates who choose to live on its wing rise at 5 a.m. for morning prayers and bustle purposefully through a day packed with studying Scripture, practicing gospel music, learning life skills, and undergoing "biblically based" therapy designed to transform them through an "instantaneous miracle." Their study regimen includes lessons in creationism and an option to "convert" out of homosexuality. When I asked Alexander Curls, on work release after three years of InnerChange, what he was taught about other faiths, he said emphatically, "I found out that a lot of good people are going *straight* to hell!"

Many inmates, however, don't join for the ideology. They do it to transfer from other parts of the prison system, and because completing InnerChange amounts to a get-out-of-jail-free card with the Parole Board: "We have a very positive relationship with the board. Sometimes they just give our inmates a green light and say, 'See you at work release,'" said Larry Furnish, InnerChange program manager at Ellsworth. Kansas has only 298 coveted work-release positions for about 9,000 total inmates; InnerChange graduates are all but guaranteed a space as well as help finding a job and housing after they get out.

Meanwhile, joining InnerChange brings about a radical change in lifestyle. The movements of the general population are highly restricted. Those who share a snack or a book will likely be written up for "dealing and trading"; during visiting hours, hugs with family members are timed. But InnerChange "members" have good prison jobs and electric guitars. They are called by their first names, hugged and told they're loved, and, because the program emphasizes reconciliation with family members, are provided much greater visitation rights—their wives can join them for Bible study and picnics.

And then there is the pizza. When a new class of inmates joins InnerChange, the staff orders 100 large pies, a fact that all 800-plus inmates at Ellsworth appear to be intimately, obsessively, aware of. "We are stretching the local Pizza Hut to its absolute capacity," InnerChange office administrator

Gale Soukup told me with a worried look, "and they're the only game in town."

Treatment and Training

Paid for in part by fees charged to the general population, InnerChange also offers substance-abuse treatment and free computer training, hot commodities in a time of budgetary woes. This year [2003], the GED program Ellsworth offers regular prisoners was cut in half, the substance-abuse program eliminated. General-population inmates are still offered a computer class through the local community college, but as it costs $150, and men who are lucky enough to land a prison job make an average of 60 cents a day, the general population's six computers sit under dust covers most days. As Issac Jarowitz, an Ellsworth inmate who isn't in Inner-Change, noted grudgingly, "The Christians do lots of stuff the state used to do, like vocational programs, but now they're only for believers."

"I tell them this is their ticket," Raymond said, gesturing to the InnerChange ID card that inmates wear on a "What Would Jesus Do?" neck chain, "to everything they need.". . .

At Ellsworth, Muslim inmates like Michael Patterson say that their practices have been restricted since InnerChange arrived. While InnerChange inmates and their families are treated to a Christmas dinner shared with prison staff, this year the Ramadan feast (which Muslim inmates must pay for and their families can't attend) was denied. InnerChange inmates engage in spontaneous prayer throughout the day, but Lakota, Muslim, and other inmates in the general population need approval to pray together. "If anyone but the Christians gets together for a prayer, security hits the panic button," Patterson said, adding that the prison's chaplain would not order Islamic texts and that an inmate who started studying Arabic was called into the warden's office. (The warden denies these reports.) To Patterson, this pattern suggests that "through a variety of avenues, the prison is trying to pressure inmates to join InnerChange to turn the whole prison into a Christian place."

That sounds paranoid, and Warden Ray Roberts (who's since become warden of another Kansas prison) said inmates are not pressured, implicitly or explicitly, to join Inner-Change. But Roberts, his deputy warden, and the prison's security chief all told me they would like the entire prison turned over to InnerChange. While walking with Raymond, an inmate suggested airbrushing a giant mural of Jesus on the side of the prison. "The state won't let that fly," Raymond said ruefully. "Wait until we take the place over.". . .

The Dangers of Faith-Based Coercion

While [Florida governor Jeb Bush's plan to establish the nation's first faith-based prison] may claim to represent several faiths, this . . . can be deceptive. No faith is monolithic and each religion has several branches, which interpret religious texts in radically different ways. . . .

True freedom of religion requires Bush to fully embrace the value of all faiths represented in the prison system. This includes equal treatment and a full array of services for Eastern religions, such as Buddhism and Hinduism, as well as unorthodox faiths such as Wicca.

Perhaps the most disturbing part of the new scheme is the potential for abusive favoritism, religious coercion and additional punishment for nonbelievers.

Wayne Besen, *Tallahassee Democrat*, June 18, 2005. www.Tallahassee.com.

InnerChange is the sort of program President Bush is promoting with faith-based initiatives, appointments, executive orders, and (so far failed) legislative attempts. The director of the White House Office for Faith-Based Initiatives says Bush has asked Attorney General John Ashcroft to investigate using InnerChange in federal prisons. Former PFM officials also lead Dare Mighty Things, which, thanks to a $2.2 million grant by the Department of Health and Human Services, now serves as a clearinghouse for faith-based and community groups applying for federal money.

It was already possible for faith groups to receive government funding to work in prisons; they simply have to separate their charity from their sermons and are forbidden to proselytize. But Bush's faith-based initiatives promote a very different theology of social action—one that he and Colson have personally experienced—that claims religion *itself* is the cure for social ills. PFM [Prison Fellowship Ministries] can receive state funds because InnerChange members enroll voluntarily, though it's hard to see the program as entirely voluntary when lifestyle and parole benefits serve as both carrot and stick. Furthermore, lifers who graduate from the InnerChange "God pod" return to cellblocks as "disciples" and are encouraged to proselytize. . . .

There's no conclusive research about whether the treatments InnerChange is experimenting with do work. The Texas Freedom Network recently reported on how Bush's faith-based initiatives have fared in that state, where they've existed the longest. It documents rampant safety violations at deregulated faith-based child-care centers and alcohol-treatment programs. Data compiled by Texas' Criminal Justice Policy Council suggests InnerChange graduates have lower rates of recidivism. But as University of Arizona sociologist Mark Chaves notes, "Prison Fellowship claims amazing success rates, but in prisons where it exists, it's often the only rehab program. We don't have comparisons between PFM and secular programs; we have comparisons between PFM and nothing."

Periodical Bibliography

The following articles have been selected to supplement the diverse views presented in this chapter.

Tom Barrett	"The Prison Revolving Door," *Conservative Truth.Org*, May 12, 2002. www.conservative truth.org.
Bill Berkowitz	"Slouching Toward Theocracy: President Bush's Faith-Based Initiative Is Doing Better than You Think," *Dissident Voice*, February 9, 2004. www.dissidentvoice.org.
Douglas A. Berman	"Having Faith in Prisons," *Sentencing Law and Policy*, October 16, 2004. www.sentencing. typepad.com.
Lorenzo Komboa Ervin	"United States: Prison: Corporate Slavery?" *Green Left Weekly*, April 25, 2005. www. greenleft.org.
Sandra Kobrin	"Dying on Our Dime: California's Prisons Are Teeming with Older Inmates Who Run Up Staggering Medical Costs," *Los Angeles Times*, June 26, 2005.
Victoria Law	"Workin' for the Man," *Clamor Magazine*, May/June 2004. www.clamormagazine.org.
Jack Leonard	"New Rule: Go to Jail, Pay to See a Nurse," *Los Angeles Times*, July 7, 2005. www.latimes. com.
Karen Miller	"Prison Labor: Some Facts and Issues," *Anarchist Black Cross Network*, July 15, 2005. www.anarchistblackcross.org.
National Center for Policy Analysis	"Using Convict Labor," *Daily Policy Digest*, March 27, 2002. www.ncpa.org.
Warren Richey	"Before High Court: Law That Allows for Religious Rights," *Christian Science Monitor*, March 21, 2005.
Geoffrey F. Segal	"Privatize Prisons, Unlock Savings," *Bluegrass Digest*, October 12, 2004.
Star Tribune	"Drug Offenders: At Last, a Wise Sentencing System," July 13, 2005.
Larry Stirling	"Prisoners Should Work," *Daily Transcript*, August 26, 2003. www.sddt.com.

Paul Street   "Race, Place, and the Perils of Prisonomics: Beyond the Big-Stick, Low-Road, and Zero-Sum Mass Incarceration Con," *Z Magazine Online*, July/August 2005. www.zmag.org.

Larry D. Thompson   "Federal Prison Industries: Fair to Business, Vital to Society," *Federal Times*, March 1, 2004. www.brook.edu.

Reginald A. Wilkinson   "Prison Jobs Teach Inmates Skills, Instill Work Ethic," *Columbus Dispatch*, August 21, 2004. www.drc.state.oh.us.

CHAPTER 4

Who Should Be Imprisoned?

Chapter Preface

Gang violence has long concerned public safety officials, who have argued that new laws are needed that would make it easier to arrest and convict gang members as well as protect witnesses to gang activities. Legislation pending in the U.S. Senate (it passed the House of Representatives) would address these concerns. The Gang Deterrence and Community Protection Act of 2005 would authorize the appropriation of nearly $80 million annually between 2006 and 2010 "to investigate and prosecute criminal street gangs and to protect witnesses and victims of gang-related crimes," according to government analysts. While supporters of the legislation contend that it will make America's streets safer, critics charge that the bill unfairly targets youths and will do nothing to deter crime.

Prisoner advocacy groups, such as Families Against Mandatory Minimums, are concerned about the legislation, which adds many new mandatory minimum penalties and "changes the definition of crime of violence to include drug trafficking crimes that involve no violence whatsoever." Jason Ziedenberg of the Justice Policy Institute contends that the law is "designed to punish young people by lowering the age at which youth can be tried as adults, funding more prosecutors, and expanding ways for the federal government to arrest, detain and imprison young people."

In contrast, supporters of the legislation argue that it will help prosecutors make successful cases against juvenile criminals. Deborah Pryce, a Republican member of the U.S. House of Representatives, argues that "passage of this gang deterrence initiative will ensure that our law enforcement officials—from cops on the beat to district attorneys in the courtroom—will have the tools they need to protect their communities." George W. Bush, writing in support of the legislation, argues that "aggressive law enforcement and tougher sentencing laws bear a good deal of the responsibility for the precipitous reduction in crime rates, especially for violent crime, over the past decade. . . . It is important to increase penalties for illegal gang activity, both to deter violence and encourage cooperation from gang members who are already conditioned to understand that they will do some prison time, but often cooperate when faced with heavier prison time."

Authors in the following chapter explore the question of who should be incarcerated in America's prisons. Imprisoning the pregnant, the mentally ill, the dying, and the very young continues to be controversial, and this debate will likely have far-reaching effects on America's prison system for years to come.

"Sound public policy dictates that serious, violent and habitual offenders need to be incarcerated to protect the public safety."

Criminal Youth Should Be Imprisoned

James C. Backstrom

James C. Backstrom is a county attorney in Hastings, Minnesota. In this viewpoint Backstrom contends that the incarceration of violent delinquents is necessary to protect public safety. He also contends that violent youth should be prosecuted as adults and sentenced by the adult justice system. Backstrom calls for less restrictions on the joint housing of adult and juvenile criminal offenders.

As you read, consider the following questions:
1. Why does Backstrom believe that housing violent juvenile offenders in adult facilities should be an option?
2. Who does Backstrom suggest should be given flexibility in decisions about housing violent juveniles in adult lockups?
3. What argument does Backstrom use to advocate for co-located juvenile and adult detention facilities?

James C. Backstrom, "A Common Sense Approach to Housing Juvenile Offenders in Adult Detention Facilities," www.co.dakota.mn.us/attorney, June 24, 2005. Reproduced by permission.

The number of serious, violent and habitual juvenile offenders in need of detention space have risen dramatically over the last 5 years in America. Census projections also reflect a growth in juvenile population of close to 20% in the United States between 1990 and 2010. In my jurisdiction, we project an increase of over 60% in the number of youth between 14–17 over the next 15 years. Even if juvenile arrest rates do not continue to grow as they have for most of the last decade, the overall number of juvenile crimes committed will likely be dramatically higher in the next 20 years given these population trends. An ominous forecast indeed.

Sound public policy dictates that serious, violent and habitual offenders need to be incarcerated to protect the public safety and provide appropriate levels of punishment and accountability. Common sense dictates that using available space in local county jails and state prisons should be an available option, subject to reasonable restrictions. In fact, adult detention facilities are probably better equipped to deal with the type of dangerous and violent juvenile offenders we are seeing today than are most juvenile detention facilities. Why shouldn't we be able to take advantage of existing detention facilities, with staffs trained in managing serious and dangerous offenders, whenever possible?

It needs to be kept in mind that many of the concerns about poor conditions and untrained staff in local jails throughout America that were part of the initial reasons which led to es-

Juvenile Arrest Rates for Violent Crime Index Offenses, 1980–2003

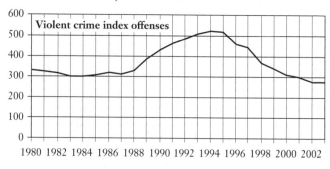

OJJDP Statistical Briefing Book, February 28, 2005. http://ojjdp.ncjrs.org.

tablishing strict regulation of juvenile detention facilities, have long been corrected. We also cannot overlook the fact that the juvenile criminal offender we see throughout America today bears little resemblance to the juvenile offender seen 20–30 years ago. We are in many circumstances dealing with sophisticated, often gang connected, juvenile criminals committing crimes of violence with dangerous weapons. There are certainly fewer reasons today to be overly concerned about segregating these hard core juvenile offenders from adult offenders as there were 25 years ago. I am not suggesting that we lock up every juvenile needing incarceration with hardened adult criminals and gang members. What I am suggesting is that local law enforcement officials be given greater flexibility in making the decision as to when and under what conditions housing serious and violent juvenile offenders in adult lockups is appropriate.

Asay. © 1999 by Creators Syndicate, Inc. Reproduced by permission.

Most modern adult jails and prisons have segregated units to allow separation of offenders by categories, such as pretrial/post-trial or men/women. These facilities can also easily segregate offenders by age groups. As one of my colleagues recently pointed out to me, juveniles aged 15–17 can be mandated by law to attend the same schools as young adults aged 18–19, but they are absolutely prohibited from being housed in a detention facility with the same young adults if they commit a crime. The fact of the matter is that in many cases the 16 year old offender was a partner with the 18 year old offender in committing the offense that led to his incarceration in the first place.

Many juvenile offenders who have committed serious and violent crime can and should be prosecuted as adults for their offenses, thereby eliminating the current legal restrictions concerning detention of these offenders in adult facilities. However, some of these offenders will not be prosecuted as adults and even those who are ultimately dealt with in adult court must be detained prior to the transfer of their case to the adult system. It certainly seems reasonable to me to allow local corrections officials the discretion to house serious, violent and habitual juvenile offenders in adult lockups if space is available and if it can be managed to insure as much segregation of juvenile and adult population as possible. Clearly, it seems appropriate in any case to allow juveniles charged or convicted of similar crimes as are young adults between 18–25 to be housed together. Co-located juvenile and adult detention facilities, utilizing shared staff and joint use of recreational/lunch and open areas, are cost effective and should also be permitted.

Some easing of federal regulatory restrictions in this area have already occurred. Last year [2005], regulations enacted by the Office of Juvenile Justice and Delinquency Prevention (OJJDP) did in fact ease some of the restrictions relating to sight and sound separation; co-location of juvenile and adult detention facilities, and immediate detention before and after court appearances. I am pleased with the direction of the leadership now being exhibited in the OJJDP, as they seek to cope with how best to deal with the new breed of juvenile criminal seen today. Clearly, a balanced approach, of appropriately holding serious, violent and habitual juvenile offenders accountable for their crimes and looking for every available means to prevent these crimes from occurring in the first place, is needed. These efforts are not incompatible—in fact they complement one another—and both protect the public safety. Common sense and sound financial planning also dictate that we further re-examine state and federal legislative restrictions dealing with the joint housing of adult and juvenile criminal offenders. Greater flexibility is needed at the local level to make determinations of when, under what conditions, and how long it is appropriate to house juvenile offenders with adults.

"Our dysfunctional juvenile justice system
. . . costs taxpayers hundreds of millions of
dollars every year, and it does not make
our communities safer."

Criminal Youth Should Not Be Imprisoned

Lenore Anderson

Lenore Anderson works with the Ella Baker Center for Human Rights. She is also the director of the Books Not Bars project. In this viewpoint she contends that the California Youth Authority, the largest youthful offender agency in the nation, is a national disgrace, costing millions of dollars and failing young people. Anderson calls for the closure of California's youth prisons, and argues for replacing them with community-based intervention in small treatment facilities. She argues that public safety requires rehabilitation, not the harsh punishment of prisons.

As you read, consider the following questions:
1. What kind of crimes bring most California youths to prison, according to Anderson?
2. What percentage of youths released from California prisons return within three years, as reported by the author?
3. According to the author, how much does California spend annually on its youth prisons?

Lenore Anderson, "Public Safety Comes with Helping Troubled Kids Change Their Lives," *Contra Costa Times*, January 30, 2005. Copyright © 2005 by Lenore Anderson. Reproduced by permission.

W hen our kids are safer, our communities are safer. Public safety comes from giving our kids in trouble the chance to turn their lives around.

But California has done just the opposite. Our dysfunctional juvenile justice system hurts public safety, hurts families, and hurts our young people in trouble. It costs taxpayers hundreds of millions of dollars every year, and it does not make our communities safer.

The California Youth Authority (CYA) is supposed to rehabilitate young people in trouble. How do you educate and rehabilitate a young person? Not with beatings. Not with sexual assault. Not with solitary confinement for months at a time. That's called abuse. And its results are predictable: nearly nine of 10 kids locked in the brutal, abusive youth prisons are back in trouble within three years. CYA is a national disgrace that is failing our kids and our communities.

[In 2005] Sen. Gloria Romero opened the door to a new dawn for California's juvenile justice system. Heeding the call of conscience, common sense and our communities, Romero introduced legislation to transform the scandal-ridden CYA. Together with Gov. [Arnold] Schwarzenegger and the new leadership of CYA also calling for dramatic reforms to support rehabilitation instead of waste and abuse, there is a way forward. This bill will do the right thing for our communities, our families and our youths in trouble.

Public safety means rehabilitation for our young people in trouble. Locking up kids in brutal prisons does not increase public safety, it does the opposite. Subjecting kids to abuse and neglect at the hands of prison guards stops them from turning their lives around. Most of the young people in CYA are there for property crimes and fighting. Kids in trouble aren't bad, they've made bad choices. And often, there is no one in their lives to help them.

Depriving kids of services they need—health care, counseling, education—makes them less able to become healthy young adults. When kids hurt themselves and hurt others in the community, we need to give them the chance to change their lives. When kids turn their lives around, our communities are peaceful and safe.

You've seen the videos: guards beating prone, vulnerable

Juvenile Crime Profile

In 2002, juveniles were involved in 1 in 10 arrests for murder (or 10% of arrests for murder), 1 in 8 arrests for a drug abuse violation, 1 in 5 arrests for a weapons violation, and 1 in 4 arrests for robbery.

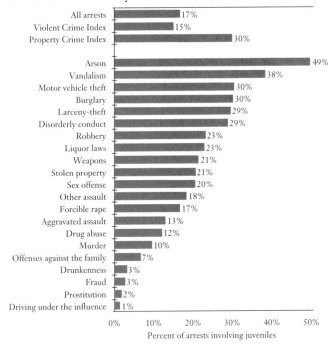

Crime in the United States 2002, Washington, DC: U.S. Government Printing Office, 2003.

young people into the ground. You've heard the horror stories: sexual assault, humiliation and violence. And you know the results: nine of 10 young people released from CYA go right back in.

Costly and Broken System

Californians spend $400 million a year on this broken system, $400 million that could be spent making our kids and our communities safer. The facts—in dozens of national studies—are clear. Community-based interventions with kids in trouble reduce crime and cost less. Locking kids up in prisons increases recidivism and violence and costs more.

The time our kids in trouble spend in the juvenile justice system should be spent in a way that benefits the community, the family, and the kids themselves. Anything else is counterproductive. Anything else is a waste of time. Anything else is a waste of our resources.

There is another way; it works and it's proven. Twenty years ago, Missouri made the changes Sen. Romero's bill advocates. And now? Missouri's recidivism rate is 8%, compared to California's 90%. In Missouri, young people who've gotten into trouble are housed in smaller facilities with better treatment and real rehabilitation. And other states are following Missouri's lead. From Louisiana to Illinois to Maryland, states across the country are transforming their dysfunctional juvenile justice systems to reduce abuse, crime and violence. If other states can do it, so can California. Sacramento's pro-prison lobby, which benefits from the way CYA is run now, may claim that CYA's problems are behind us. They will claim that real reform "goes too far."

But the facts tell a different story. This month [January 2005], the state Inspector General released an "Accountability Audit" of CYA reporting that widespread abuses continue throughout the CYA system. Just days before the report's release, youths at both the Ventura facility for girls and the Chino boys' facility separately filed suit for sexual assault by CYA staff.

Sen. Romero's bill gets to the root of the problem by closing the youth prisons, replacing them with effective programs, and making sure skilled counselors—not prison guards—are rehabilitating our young people in trouble.

We can prioritize the safety of our communities. We can close these abusive and wasteful youth prisons and make our young people safer, stronger and healthier. The legislature should pass Sen. Romero's bill, and the governor should sign it.

"Denying terminally ill women in prison the chance to spend their last days with their families is unacceptable."

Dying Prisoners Should Receive Compassionate Release

Rashida Edmondson

Rashida Edmondson is a legal advocate with the human rights organization Justice Now. In this viewpoint Edmondson argues that California's prison system could save hundreds of thousands of dollars by offering compassionate release to terminally ill prisoners. Keeping dying prisoners locked away from their families is cruel, Edmondson asserts. Dying prisoners who pose no further threat to society routinely spend their last days shackled to their beds under 24-hour guard. Edmonson argues that continued incarceration of such incapacitated persons is illogical and unnecessary, particularly when prisoners' families are willing to provide end-of-life care.

As you read, consider the following questions:

1. According to the author, how close to death must a prisoner be to qualify for compassionate release?
2. Which authorities have to first approve a dying prisoner's release, as related by Edmondson?
3. Who has the final approval in granting compassionate release to a dying prisoner, according to Edmondson?

"I don't want my mommy to die in that place by herself. I want her to come home first so we can hug her and take lots of pictures together. Will you please let her come home before God takes her to His home? Please?"

—Karma Dias, 10

During the holidays, Karma Dias, like most of us, will be spending time with her family and loved ones. But unless a judge shows compassion, Karma's mother will not be there, because she is dying in prison.

Compassionate Release Saves Money

The state could save hundreds of thousands by sending Karma's mother, and others like her, home. After all, it can cost a small fortune to keep a terminally ill person in prison. As our state [California] fights the worst budget crisis in its history, taxpayers are carrying the burden of keeping dying, medically incapacitated people locked away from their families. Meanwhile, the budget for the Department of Corrections budget has been spared from any cuts.

Karma's mother, Beverly Dias, 51, is dying at Valley State Prison for Women in Chowchilla (Madera County). She has 20 months left on a 6-year sentence for possession of 6.3 grams of cocaine. Dias is suffering from a combination of liver cancer and cirrhosis of the liver caused by hepatitis C. The only treatment remaining for her is to undergo a liver transplant. But she has been denied transplant eligibility by the transplant team at the University of California at Davis. No female prisoner in the history of California has ever been allowed to obtain an organ transplant. Without the transplant, doctors have declared that Dias will die in the next six months.

Dias is in constant pain and requires significant pain medication to function at a very basic level. She is constantly fatigued and sleeps 14 or 15 hours a day. She is so incapacitated that she is unable to walk to the cafeteria for meals, instead relying on cellmates to bring food for her.

Working with our nonprofit organization [Justice Now], Dias applied to get out of prison early under California's compassionate release law, which allows the early release of prisoners who have less than six months to live and who pose no threat to society. The intent of this law is to allow prisoners to spend their last days with their families and not alone in prison.

Why Should We Care?

Dying in prison is what inmates dread most. They fear spending their last hours in agony, alone, separated from family outside and from friends within prison walls. Yet those worst dreams can come true for over 2,500 prisoners a year, who die manacled in hospitals or in prison infirmaries.

Why should we care where and how inmates die? This question is implicit whenever prison hospice or compassionate release is discussed in the media and with politicians. Many people would respond that we should care simply because prisoners are human beings and humane treatment is simply the right thing to do. Many Americans, however, feel that convicted murderers, rapists, child molesters, and drug dealers deserve whatever they get. If they die suffering, in pain and alone, so be it.

But turning a blind eye is not an option. American courts have forcefully distinguished punishment from brutality and have repeatedly affirmed society's responsibility to provide a community level of care for prisoners. . . .

Under the constant scrutiny of prisoners and advocate groups, federal and state institutions, which fail to honor their responsibility to provide adequate care, risk legal peril and fiscal liability. Consequently, excellent medical care in corrections is well aligned with society's (read taxpayers') best interests.

Ira R. Byock, "Dying Well in Corrections: Why Should We Care?" *Journal of Correctional HealthCare*, 2002.

Last week [December 2003], after previously denying her release, the director of the California Department of Corrections, Edward Alameida, reconsidered and recommended Dias for compassionate release. We credit his change of heart to widespread support from the community. Now it is all in the hands of the judge who originally sentenced Dias, Rene Navarro, to approve her release. [Dias was granted compassionate release].

Confining the Dying Is Cruel

The plea of Beverly's daughter Karma is the plea of all children who wish for their parents to come home to die. We are working with dozens of other women who will die in prison. Their prospects of spending their last days at home are minuscule. In the past two months, two terminally ill women whom we worked with have died in the custody of the corrections department, despite qualifying for compassionate release. They died hospitalized and bed ridden, shackled to their beds and guarded 24 hours a day by security officers earning overtime pay. These deaths followed a 10-day period in July, when three other women we represented died in similar fashion.

Denying terminally ill women in prison the chance to spend their last days with their families is unacceptable and thwarts the intent behind the compassionate release law.

Beverly Dias' story, while one of hope, highlights our prison system's illogical policies that result in enormous waste of money and human potential. The fact that our state is spending scarce resources to confine dying prisoners is especially troublesome in these rough economic times.

The approaching holiday season is a time for family, compassion and goodwill. At this time, Dias needs to go home. It is cruel and inhumane to deny a 10-year-old child's simple wish that her mother come home to die.

"Rather than being shackled to a bed in a strange hospital, [the prisoner] stays in familiar surroundings."

Prison Hospice Care Meets the Needs of Dying Prisoners

Anne M. Seidlitz

The National Prison Hospice Association promotes hospice care for terminally ill prisoners. In this viewpoint Anne M. Seidlitz explains that with the rising prison population has come an increase in aging and dying prisoners in need of end-of-life care. Seidlitz contend that the prison hospice model provides a cost-effective means of meeting the needs of dying prisoners. Part of the savings and benefits of the program are brought about through involvement of healthy prisoners, who are trained in end-of-life caretaking tasks. In addition, the organization notes, many prisoners request to sign "Do Not Resuscitate" directives, saving additional money otherwise spent on life-prolonging measures.

As you read, consider the following questions:
1. Why are healthy prisoners transferred to the prison medical center, in Seidlitz's view?
2. According to the author, what illness most accounts for the increase in dying prisoners?
3. What is one beneficial effect of the Inmate Hospice Program on healthy prisoners, as related by the author?

Anne M. Seidlitz, "FMC-Fort Worth, a Prison Hospice Model for the Future," *NPHA News*, vol. 1, Winter 1996/1997. Copyright © 1996 by the National Prison Hospice Association. Reproduced by permission.

The Federal Medical Center at Fort Worth, Texas, built in 1956, is one of six federally run prison medical centers. Correctional medical centers like FMC-Fort Worth remain invisible spots on an American landscape in which the realities of prison life are largely obscured from the public's view. . . .

Except for the coils of razor wire that top its high fences and armed vehicles at its perimeter, FMC-Fort Worth is hardly distinguishable as a prison. But inside its walls nearly 1400 male inmates are incarcerated, approximately 580 of whom have been transferred from other prison facilities not designed to care for them. These inmates have a spectrum of illnesses ranging from chronic asthma to full-blown AIDS, making ambulatory to long-term care a necessity.

Healthy Prisoners Help

The 800 or so healthy inmates at Fort Worth are incarcerated there for the services they can provide at the Medical Center. One capacity in which the healthy population supports the hospitalized inmates is through their participation in a special program at Fort Worth, the Inmate Hospice Program. This program was introduced in 1994, and has since become a model for hospice in the corrections environment. . . .

While attitudes toward death and dying are changing in our communities, at the same time the number of inmates dying in prisons is rising. This fact has been attributed to the increasing number of AIDS cases in the prison population, and a trend of tougher sentencing laws that began with the Sentencing Reform Act of 1987, and which has resulted in a burgeoning number of older inmates serving longer sentences. . . .

Cost

Since its inception in 1994 the Hospice Program has proven to consistently reduce the costs of caring for its terminally ill inmates. A number of features of the Hospice Program contribute to its cost benefits. The central contributing factor is the self-containment of the program within the prison's Medical Center. As nearly all the medical and support needs of the hospice patients are met in the Long Term Care Unit, the number of outside trips to hospitals has decreased dramatically, saving the considerable expense involved. The patient benefits as well: rather than being shackled to a bed in a strange hospital, he stays in familiar surroundings with his Care Teams providing the support and care he is accustomed to.

Dying Humanely in Prison

The over two million individuals in this country's prisons and jails represent an aging population with multiple chronic medical problems. Many prisoners are destined to die while incarcerated. Correctional systems have a responsibility to attend to end of life issues, which include advance directives and management of pain and other symptoms of terminal conditions. Although many jails and prisons choose to transfer patients to community facilities for end of life care, patients can be cared for in the correctional setting in a secure, competent, compassionate manner. Close cooperation between custody and medical staff is necessary for the success of any correctional end of life care program. With the active participation of all those involved, terminally ill prisoners who will not be released can be provided a humane end of life experience within the correctional setting.

Joseph Bick, "Providing Palliative Care for Incarcerated Patients," *HEPP Report*, May 2003.

Another cost-saving effect of the Hospice Program at Fort Worth is a marked reduction in the "heroic measures" that are often taken as the patient's vital functions weaken. After being better prepared psychologically and spiritually for death through the hospice approach, inmates more often request to sign "Do Not Resuscitate" orders, asking not to be put on ventilators or other means of life support towards the end. This saves the prison a huge amount of money that would otherwise be spent on procedures that have been increasingly viewed as undesirable from the standpoints of both patients and care-givers.

A vital component of the Hospice Program at FMC-Fort Worth is the Inmate Hospice Volunteer Program, made up of approximately fifty volunteers from the healthy prison population who perform a spectrum of functions as part of the Care Teams. Many of the services they perform, from range of motion exercises to psychological support as "buddies" of the sick inmates, would otherwise be done by either an expanded nursing staff or outside groups. Again, the Hospice Program's utilization of existing prison resources has proven to streamline the costs of caring for its most critically ill inmates while providing these inmates with a consistent and reliable support network. . . .

The Hospice Program has had a positive impact on Fort Worth's healthy inmate population. The program sends out the message that prison officials and its Health Care staff are attending to the needs of even the sickest inmates. Much of this message is disseminated through the inmate volunteers. After an intensive three-week training program educating them about a wide range of health care and hospice issues, the volunteers are then prepared to work closely with the medical staff, and see first-hand that adequate care is being given to each patient. The positive picture that they bring back out to the general prison population cuts down on the customary resentment and distrust felt when an inmate dies.

"The country's prisons and jails have become the default mental health system. Somewhere between two and four hundred thousand mentally ill people are incarcerated."

Mentally Ill Criminals Should Not Be Imprisoned

Joanne Mariner

Joanne Mariner is a lawyer with Human Rights Watch, an organization dedicated to protecting the human rights of people around the world. In this viewpoint, based on a Human Rights Watch report on prisoners with mental illness, Mariner contends that imprisonment of the mentally ill is abusive. She blames the increased incarceration of the mentally ill to the "deinstitutionalization" effort during the 1960s, which released thousands of institutionalized mentally ill people back into communities without adequate support services. She argues that many of the imprisoned mentally ill could be safely cared for in community-based mental health treatment programs.

As you read, consider the following questions:

1. According to the American Psychiatric Association, what kinds of serious mental disorders affect many American prisoners?
2. Are U.S. prison staff trained in effective mental health intervention, in the author's view?
3. As related by Mariner, what kind of prison conditions are mentally ill persons exposed to in America's prisons?

U.S. prisons and jails, packed with over two million inmates, hold many people that society would be wise to keep elsewhere. With state budgets bankrupted by the high costs of mass incarceration, the need to reconsider the draconian sentences meted out to nonviolent drug offenders has never been more obvious.

There is, moreover, another sizeable group of prisoners for which wholesale imprisonment is even less appropriate: the mentally ill. Prisoners with mental illness frequently endure violence, exploitation and extortion at the hands of other inmates, and neglect and mistreatment by prison staff. Not only is the experience of imprisonment counter-therapeutic for such prisoners, many mental health experts believe that it dramatically increases their chances of psychiatric breakdown.

Despite good reasons to limit the incarceration of the mentally ill, their numbers behind bars continue to grow. Over the past few decades, the country's prisons and jails have become the default mental health system. Somewhere between two and four hundred thousand mentally ill people are incarcerated, several times more than the number of people living in mental institutions.

The results, from a therapeutic, humanitarian, and human rights perspective, are appalling. "We are literally drowning in patients," explains one California prison psychiatrist, "running around trying to put our fingers in the bursting dikes, while hundreds of men continue to deteriorate psychiatrically before our eyes."

"Criminalizing" the Mentally Ill

The American Psychiatric Association, in a study published in 2000, concluded that as many as one in five prisoners was seriously mentally ill, with up to 5 percent being actively psychotic at any given moment. It also estimated that over 700,000 mentally ill people were processed through prison or jail each year. The mental disorders affecting these prisoners include such serious illnesses as schizophrenia, bipolar disorder, and major depression.

There are no national data on historical rates of mental illness among prisoners, but state information suggests that the proportion of mentally ill prisoners has grown significantly.

Human Rights Watch, in a [2003 report], traces this increase to the inadequacy of the country's mental heath services.

From Hospital to Prison?

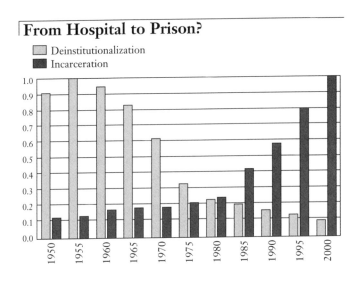

Tom Hamilton, "Guilty of Being Ill—Does the Punishment Fit the Crime?" Report presented at APA's fall component meetings, September 2003.

With the "deinstitutionalization" effort that began in the 1960s, hundreds of thousands of mentally ill men and women were released from state institutions. These people escaped grim conditions and sometimes brutal treatment. They largely did not, however, obtain proper care after their release. Rather than receiving continuing mental health treatment, mentally ill people were released to communities that had made little or no accommodation for their care.

While states cut funding for mental hospitals, they did not make commensurate increases in the budgets for community-based mental health services. Chronically underfunded, the country's mental health system does not reach anywhere near the number of people who need it.

Left untreated and unstable, mentally ill people enter the criminal justice system when they break the law. And given the punitive criminal justice policies of the past few decades, they often face long stays behind bars.

In a series of disturbing passages, the recent Human

Rights Watch report described the abuses endured by the mentally ill while incarcerated.

To begin with, few prisons or jails have sufficient numbers of trained staff to accommodate prisoners' mental health needs. As a result, many mentally ill prisoners go untreated, or receive treatment that is extremely limited in both quantity and quality.

From other prisoners, who label them "dings" or "bugs," the mentally ill are vulnerable to assault, sexual abuse, exploitation, and extortion. From security staff, who frequently dismiss their symptoms as faking or manipulation, they may face physical abuse and mental harassment. Human Rights Watch cited numerous cases of correctional officers who taunted mentally ill prisoners, deliberately provoked them, physically mistreated them, used force against them maliciously, or turned a blind eye to abuses against them by others.

Viewing mentally ill prisoners as difficult and disruptive, correctional staff also frequently place them in barren high-security solitary confinement units. Held in small, sometimes windowless cells, these inmates are deprived of nearly all human interaction and have extremely limited mental stimulus.

In such harsh conditions, some mentally ill prisoners deteriorate so severely that they must be removed to hospitals for acute psychiatric care. But after their condition stabilizes, they are frequently returned to the same segregation units until the next psychiatric episode occurs.

The Need for Reform

The immeasurable human suffering caused by the mass incarceration of the mentally ill is not only inhumane, it is unnecessary. While some dangerous offenders must be confined to protect society, there are many low-level, nonviolent offenders with mental illness who could be safely diverted into community-based mental health treatment programs. By reducing the overall number of mentally ill prisoners, such programs would also free up prison resources that could be used to remedy the generally low quality of prison mental health care. . . .

It is national shame that our prisons and jails serve as mental institutions. It reflects a lack of planning, a failure of public commitment, and a single-minded focus on punishment.

"The mental hospital now looks like a prison. Three years ago, a 14-foot-tall fence topped with razor wire was erected around the hospital to better ensure public safety."

Caring for Mentally Ill Criminals Outside of Prison Is Dangerous

Jim Doyle and Peter Fimrite

Jim Doyle and Peter Fimrite are reporters with the *San Francisco Chronicle*. In this viewpoint the authors outline some of the problems that occur when the criminally insane are sentenced to state hospitals. The California hospital they write about has become what they characterize as a "holding pen" for criminally inclined mentally ill patients. The authors contend that the hospital is overcrowded and understaffed, conditions that are dangerous for both staff and patients. Moreover, hospital workers are not adequately trained to manage violent offenders, the authors argue.

As you read, consider the following questions:

1. What are some of the problems with mixing the criminally insane with other patients, in the authors' view?
2. As cited by Doyle and Fimrite, what percentage of the hospital's patients has been committed by state criminal courts?
3. According to the authors, how much time is spent in training nursing staff on how to deal with assaultive behavior at the mental health facility?

In California's mental health system . . . criminally inclined, often violent patients are now in the majority at state hospitals—and the hospitals are ill-equipped to handle them.

The problem has reached a critical stage at Napa State Hospital, which has a severe employee shortage and where staff members are given only rudimentary training on how to deal with criminal behavior.

With more than 100 job vacancies at the hospital, the nursing staff has barely enough time to clothe, feed and medicate patients, let alone deal with violent outbursts. . . .

In the last four years, the once sleepy campus-style hospital has become a holding pen for men and women incompetent to stand trial on criminal charges or found not guilty of crimes by reason of insanity.

Hospital or Prison?

It is a dramatic shift from its founding purpose: Since 1875, the hospital had mainly served mentally ill patients committed by civil courts.

The mental hospital now looks like a prison. Three years ago, a 14-foot-tall fence topped with razor wire was erected around the hospital to better ensure public safety. Nine kiosks with armed guards are manned 24 hours a day at the medium-security complex. . . .

Any facility that houses the criminally insane is an inherently dangerous place. But current and former Napa State Hospital staff members say the way the hospital is run heightens the risk of harm to both staff and patients:

• Patient wards are overcrowded. In some units, four and sometimes five patients are housed in small dormitory rooms. Murderers and other violent patients are routinely placed in wards with highly vulnerable patients, including the elderly.

• Napa State requires nurses and psychiatric technicians to work overtime, including 16-hour "double shifts," due to a staff shortage. To maintain minimal staff levels, administrators also rely on unlicensed and temporary workers.

• The nursing staff has minimal training to deal with the hospital's increasing number of violent male patients. At night, nurses and psychiatric technicians are known to lock

Part Prison, Part Hospital

Oregon State Hospital houses its largest, toughest program in old, crumbling buildings . . .

It's a captive, often-incompatible meeting of sick people and dangerous criminals dispatched by Oregon's courts. Most have been charged with crimes and found guilty except for insanity. Their crimes range from murders to misdemeanors. . . .

Critics call it a de facto prison.

Defenders call it a caring hospital of last resort.

People in both camps have a point because the forensic program has a split personality—part prison, part hospital.

It's a place where therapists encourage troubled patients to bare their feelings in group therapy sessions, and it's a place where clanging metal gates and tall fences reinforced with razor wire prevent escapes.

Security coexists with therapy amid daily routines:

- Patients have staff escorts when they venture off their assigned wards.
- Visitors undergo metal detectors to prevent weapons from being slipped in to patients.
- Surveillance cameras cover visiting room activity.
- Security staff check mailed-in packages for dozens of items patients are not allowed to have, including cameras, metal combs, pagers, credit cards and chewing gum. . . .

Amid daily work routines, staff members adhere to a central operating principle: They are dealing with mental patients, not prisoners.

Still the dual nature of the forensic program makes for a tough balancing act.

Statesman Journal, December 26, 2004. www.statesmanjournal.com.

themselves in the unit's nursing station where they attend to paperwork.

• Patient-on-patient assaults, a near daily occurrence, are rarely investigated and only occasionally referred for prosecution. . . . Nurses say they can barely keep up with assaults, let alone the prison-style intimidation. Certain violations, they say, get swept under the rug.

"There is just not enough staff to supervise that many violent people," said a registered nurse in a forensic unit. . . . She did not want her name used out of fear for her job. "I've personally been assaulted several times there, and I know quite a few other staff members who have also."

Criminally Insane Predators

Since June 1995, the number of patients committed to Napa State Hospital by the state criminal courts has more than doubled—from 337 patients to 853. Civilly committed patients, who are housed separately, now make up only 21 percent of the hospital's total population of 1,081. . . .

While patient abuse by staff—a significant problem a generation ago—has been curtailed, insiders say the hospital corridors are made increasingly dangerous by criminally insane predators roaming the hallways. Often, it is the passive, emotionally vulnerable patients originally committed for minor crimes who pay the price. . . .

Workers are required to take a three-day course on how to deal with assaultive behavior—but most nurses at Napa State Hospital are trained to treat mental illness, not violence. In contrast, state prison guards must graduate from a rigorous, 16-week training academy covering everything from weapons training and first aid to strategies for handling violent offenders.

| *"The recent practice of locking up more women who are mothers of minor children is extremely damaging and costly for society. It damages both the children during their developmental stages and their parent."*

Mothers Should Not Be Imprisoned

Jackie Crawford

Jackie Crawford is the director of the Nevada Department of Corrections. In this viewpoint Crawford argues that imprisoning women with dependent children breaks down family ties and causes harm to the children and society as a whole. According to Crawford, children with a parent in prison experience higher rates of delinquency and teen pregnancy. Alternative sentencing and community-based treatment would be more humane, effective, and less costly, the author contends.

As you read, consider the following questions:
1. According to the author, what are some of the circumstances that keep imprisoned mothers from receiving visits from their children? What are some of the problems caused by loss of parental contact?
2. What percentage of children of incarcerated parents is likely to become incarcerated themselves, according to information cited by the author?
3. According to Crawford, what programs are most effective as alternatives to incarceration for women offenders?

Jackie Crawford, "Alternative Sentencing Necessary for Female Inmates with Children," *Corrections Today*, vol. 65, June 2003, p. 8. Copyright © 2003 by the American Correctional Association, Inc. Reproduced by permission.

The reason that there has been such an increase in incarcerated females is the change in sentencing laws passed by legislatures during the past two decades—the so-called sentencing reform acts. It used to be that judges were inclined to restrict the use of incarceration of both men and women who had family responsibilities. But now, the sentencing reform guidelines make that either less likely or impossible in some cases. According to researchers John Hagan and Ronit Dinovitzer, in recent years, judges seem to be imposing the same standards on men and women by disregarding the greater family responsibilities of women for children in families. "The result is that the number of mothers of children who are being incarcerated is growing . . . and researchers increasingly express concern about this."

Collateral Damage

This raises a particularly serious concern for the long run because of the implications, not only for the children and their parents, but also for society as a whole. In today's language, the concern is about what kind of "collateral damage" is being done to the children of these imprisoned parents. Because of the growing numbers of mothers being incarcerated for years at a time, there is a group of individuals whose lives have been grossly interfered with that few people stop to think about—the young people. Their lives are disrupted and damaged by the separation from imprisoned mothers and fathers. It is especially true when a mother is incarcerated that it is often uncertain who will care for her children. When fathers are incarcerated, there is usually a mother left at home to care for the children. However, when mothers are incarcerated, there is not usually a father in the home.

This situation is further exacerbated by the fact that there are fewer women's prisons. Therefore, there is a greater risk that female offenders will be incarcerated at a greater distance from their children than males. According to Hagan and Dinovitzer, an average female inmate is more than 160 miles farther from her family than a male inmate and at least half the children of imprisoned mothers have either not seen or not visited their mothers since they were incarcerated. This low rate of contact between mother and child tends to break down family relationships, which causes psychological and emotional damage both to the child and to the incarcerated mother. This low rate of contact has another negative consequence, as studies show that the maintenance of strong family ties during incarceration tends to lower recidivism rates, and that "on the whole, prison inmates with family ties during imprisonment do better on release than those without them."

The damage done to the children is probably more serious than to the adult when a parent is imprisoned. A number of children display symptoms of post-traumatic stress disorder, namely depression, feelings of anger and guilt, flashbacks about their mother's crimes or arrests, and the experience of hearing their mother's voice. Hagan and Dinovitzer go on to say that "the trauma that these children experience due to an early separation from their primary caregiver and the difficult life that follows impact their mental health." Children of incarcerated mothers display other negative effects such as school-related difficulties, depression, low self-esteem, aggressive behavior and general emotional dysfunction. Hagan and Dinovitzer note one study of children of incarcerated mothers in which 40 percent of the boys ages 12 to 17 were delinquent, while the rate of teenage pregnancy among female children was 60 percent.

The general effects on a child who is separated from an incarcerated parent, especially the mother, is that this circumstance tends to interfere with the child's ability to successfully master developmental tasks and overcome the effects of such an enduring trauma of parent-child separation. Frequently, the children are often left with a caregiving arrangement that is inadequate, unreliable or irregular, and this causes further long-term damage to the development of the character and personality of the child. Because of these deprivations and traumas, children of incarcerated parents may be six times more likely than their counterparts to become incarcerated themselves, according to Hagan and Dinovitzer. This unwanted, unanticipated effect is part of the collateral damage not only to the child, but also for society as a whole because of the intergenerational transmission of risks of imprisonment.

Some may think that the children of drug abusers, alcoholics and property criminals might be better off growing up without their influence, but this is not what studies show. It is more likely that imprisonment of parents is more harmful to children, even when they come from dysfunctional families. Imprisoning parents is more likely to compound, than to mitigate, pre-existing family problems. Once the parent is removed from the household, the quality of alternative care arrangements for the children may be worse, which only enhances the trauma of separation.

Special Needs of Female Offenders

Upon intake, there are gender-specific needs prison staff must perform for accurate and meaningful classification regarding female offenders, such as needs related to children, histories of spousal and child sexual abuse, job training, etc. Management styles for administrators of women's facilities need to differ in order to address female offenders' behavioral patterns since the inmates tend to be more emotional and develop more social relationships within prison than men do. It is more appropriate to employ alternatives to incarceration for more female offenders, as they tend to be nonviolent and not a threat to society. On the other hand, they have more emotional and mental health problems that need to be addressed in a holistic manner and these can be better met in small, community-based settings. More comprehensive programs are needed for women that address their past histories of abuse and their own substance abuse.

Programs that are most effective include a combination of substance abuse programs, work training programs, parenting classes, child visitation programs, work release and a variety of transition, aftercare, education and health programs. The most appropriate staff for facilities for female offenders are women who provide strong female role models. Female offenders need to be able to form supportive peer networks and have programs that address their particular experiences as victims of child sexual abuse, domestic violence and as parents of children who have been in negative relationships with men. They need to have their substance abuse habits addressed along with mental health services to address their past histories of abuse, low self-esteem and tendencies to get into negative and self-defeating relationships. When this combination of needs is addressed for female offenders, there is a likelihood of recidivism reduction.

Children with Parents in Prison

State prisoners who were parents were less likely to be violent offenders (44 percent) than inmates without children (51 percent), the report said. Three-quarters of state prisoners who were parents had a prior conviction, and a majority (56 percent) had previously been incarcerated. On average, the imprisoned parents expected to serve more than six-and-a-half years in state prison and eight-and-a-half years in federal prison. . . .

A majority of both fathers (57 percent) and mothers (54 percent) reported never having had a personal visit with their children since their admission to state prison. More than 60 percent of the parents in state prisons reported being held more than 100 miles from their last place of residence.

Christopher J. Mumola, "Incarcerated Parents and Their Children," Bureau of Justice Statistics, August 2000.

So if social leaders and policy-makers were to think about this situation, they would understand that the recent practice of locking up more women who are mothers of minor children is extremely damaging and costly for society. It damages both the children during their developmental stages and their parent. The children are more likely to enter into the criminal justice system than their peers who do not have incarcerated parents, and the mother who is separated from her child is more likely to recidivate herself. Therefore, the current practice is actually one that is geared to unintentionally send more people into the criminal justice system, potentially to be locked up, at an exponential rate. This would cost society untold billions within the next generation. The current cost for incarcerated inmates in our nation is more than $30 billion per year. Multiply that by four or five, and it can be seen that this will lead to an out-of-control situation.

It is ironic that the answer to decreasing the problem of the growing incarceration of women is both more humane, more effective and less costly. The solution is to put as many nonviolent, drug-related offenders into halfway houses or community-based drug treatment programs that address their past histories, as well as their current behaviors, and teaches them accountability. This leads to greater success rates and keeps offenders in the community closer to their children, giving them a much better chance of not re-entering that revolving door. With greater accessibility to their children, both mother and child will have a much better chance of learning healthy behaviors and knitting together a family life that is positive upon release. Some of the research and training that the National Institute of Corrections has sponsored has contributed to these findings and the indications of improved and more effective policies are self-evident.

"Women prisoners in the state of California, like others throughout the country, will labor in shackles, will be fed substandard diets while pregnant, and will be denied pain medications and antibiotics after delivery, even if they have C-sections.

Imprisoning Pregnant Women Harms Unborn Children

Ayelet Waldman

In this viewpoint Ayelet Waldman contends that the treatment of imprisoned pregnant women is harmful to their unborn children. She argues on behalf of legislation before the California Senate that would exempt pregnant prisoners from being routinely shackled during delivery and recovery after giving birth. The author contends that the harsh treatment of pregnant prisoners, and the denial of their special nutritional needs, constitutes child abuse. The California Senate had not acted on AB 478 at the time this viewpoint was written.

As you read, consider the following questions:

1. How many states in addition to California permit the chaining of women in labor to hospital beds, according to the author?
2. In the author's view, how much additional annual cost to the prison system would be incurred if AB 478 passes the California Senate?

Anna (not her real name), a prisoner at Valley State Prison for Women in Chowchilla, Calif., spent the last two weeks of her pregnancy in preterm labor, shackled to a hospital bed. If she needed to use the bathroom, or even turn over, she had to beg permission of the officer on duty. Given these strict security arrangements, you might assume that Anna was a terrorist, a murderer, some kind of hardened criminal at risk for escape. No. Anna is a minimum-security prisoner currently serving an approximately 18-month sentence for drug possession and probation violation, and according to Karen Shain, administrative director of Legal Services for Prisoners with Children, the treatment she received was routine. Whether they are violent offenders or not—and approximately 66 percent of incarcerated women in the United States are not—pregnant prisoners are subject to the same dehumanizing treatment.

On May 16 [2005], the California state Assembly passed A.B. 478 (49 to 26 with 5 abstentions), and sent it on to the state Senate.[1]

The bill provides that, unless necessary, prisoners "shall not be shackled by the wrists, ankles, or both during labor, including during transport to the hospital, during delivery, and while in recovery after giving birth." It's hard to believe that this doesn't go without saying. But according to Robin Levi, human rights director at Justice Now, a women prisoners' rights organization, California and at least 20 other states permit the chaining of laboring women to hospital beds, even when their attending physicians would prefer that they get up and walk around, or just shift from side to side. She also told me that women who return to prison from the hospital days after having Caesarean sections are routinely denied pain medication and even antibiotics.

Another part of A.B. 478 requires that pregnant women receive "necessary nutrition and vitamins, information and education, and regular dental cleanings." The necessity of supplying prenatal vitamins is obvious, although the fact that it needs to be legislated is troubling. According to a study by the University of Alabama, gum disease can cause both pre-

1. A.B. 478 was still in the California Senate when this viewpoint was written.

mature birth and low birth weight, preventable by a simple teeth cleaning during the second trimester. Still, providing teeth cleanings to prisoners might strike some as unnecessary. After all, only 35.2 percent of Americans have dental insurance; why should a prisoner receive what someone who hasn't committed a crime does not? Because by incarcerating these mothers, and making it impossible for them to seek medical care outside the prison system, we have assumed responsibility for their infants. We owe them this minimal standard of care.

No Dental Care

But what we actually do is far short of that. Take Judith (also not her real name), another Valley State prisoner, incarcerated on a probation violation for saying "F— you" to a case worker in a drug treatment program. Desperate to get into California's Community Prisoner Mother Program, where children can stay with their mothers for up to six years in a residential facility, she was informed that she would first have to have an oral exam to prove that she had no dental problems, not even a cavity. (Karen Shain believes this requirement exists as a filtering mechanism more than anything else because there are so many women who qualify for the program.) In a cruel paradox, dental care is not provided to applicants to the program, other than extractions. No fillings, no cleanings. Nothing. Judith had myriad dental problems. According to Shain, in order to be with her baby she had to have 15 teeth removed. She had no other choice.

It is hard to figure out the philosophy, either articulated or presumed, behind treating women and their babies this way. As much as prison maternity policy can sometimes feel like an especially cruel and institutionalized form of child abuse, I doubt the individuals running the prisons of this country are consciously trying to harm the infants born to prisoners. Cristina Rathbone, an investigative journalist whose book "A World Apart: Women, Prison, and Life Behind Bars" follows the lives of four prisoners at MCI-Framingham, a Massachusetts women's prison, attributes the treatment of women in prison to a kind of unconscious cruelty. Because women are a minority in prisons, they suffer the rules that have been invented for violent men. California Department of Corrections policies simply state that all inmates must be shackled when being transported to and from the hospital and while in their hospital beds. No exceptions have ever been made, not even for terminally ill or comatose prisoners, so none are made for pregnant and laboring prisoners. Until Assembly member Sally Lieber, the author and sponsor of the bill, took an interest, it simply never occurred to anyone in a position of authority that there was anything wrong with that.

Prison Pregnancy Perils

Miscarriage and stillbirth rates are high in jail and prison: one California study reported rates as much as 50 times higher than in the outside community. The full extent of the problem is unknown, however, because data on pregnancy outcomes is not systematically collected or published. What is known is that typical prison conditions compound women's medical problems and place healthy women in jeopardy. Women may suffer from such chronic illnesses as asthma, diabetes, high blood pressure, HIV/AIDS, and addiction to alcohol or drugs. Serious overcrowding exposes pregnant women to communicable diseases.

Prenatal vitamins and nutritious diets are not routinely provided, but prescription medication contraindicated during pregnancy often is. Few jails or prisons have an obstetrician/gynecologist on site.

For at least twenty-five years, advocates have been reporting that many jails and prisons do not initiate the process to transfer a pregnant woman to an outside hospital until she goes into labor. Administrative delays result in women laboring in police cars or giving birth in the infirmary or even in their cells. . . .

Women who escape this fate and make it to a hospital often suffer a final indignity: they are handcuffed, shackled around the belly, and placed in leg irons when being transported to receive medical care, even when they are in active labor, and are typically shackled to the hospital bed when they give birth and for the duration of their stay. . . .

In most cases, women who survive the obstacle course of pregnancy behind bars to give birth are separated immediately from their newborns and returned to prison.

Rachel Roth, *Justiced Denied: Violations of Women's Reproductive Rights in the United States Prison System*, 2004.

Lieber's consciousness about the issue was raised when she visited Valley State, met pregnant women prisoners, and saw that their families had to bring them bags of food to supplement their inadequate diets. Lieber says that if other legislators talked to these women and saw the conditions they lived in, they would vote for the bill. Instead of viewing corrections as an opportunity to prove how tough they are, they might realize that, as Lieber says, "there is no excuse for the state of California to have starving, shackled pregnant women behind bars."

Prenatal Nourishment Begrudged

It does seem that the way we treat all prisoners, especially women, speaks of something more than mere indifference. There seems to be a kind of retributive force at work that compelled 26 Republicans to oppose this bill. The bill asks no more, after all, than that pregnant women be treated with a modicum of decency, and that the state take a nearly token interest in the well-being of their babies. Republican opposition was, ostensibly, on fiscal grounds. This despite the fact that the Assembly appropriations analysis reported that the costs associated with the bill are "minor" and "absorbable," less than $50,000 a year. Pending the passage of A.B. 478, a pregnant woman in a California prison is entitled to no more nutritional supplementation than one extra carton of milk per day. The new bill seeks to give her a daily prenatal vitamin, slightly more balanced meals, and single teeth cleaning during her pregnancy. And yet even Republican Assembly member Bill Emmerson, an orthodontist, begrudged pregnant prisoners and their babies this low-cost protection, voting against it in committee. (Assembly member Emmerson refused to comment for this article.)

Why are the architects of the family-values agenda so eager to punish into the next generation? What is being served by seeking, quite literally, a tooth for a tooth?

Now the California Senate must vote on its version of Bill 478, and then it is up to Gov. Arnold Schwarzenegger to decide whether to sign the bill or to veto it. Until this happens, women prisoners in the state of California, like others throughout the country, will labor in shackles, will be fed substandard diets while pregnant, and will be denied pain medications and antibiotics after delivery, even if they have C-sections. And their babies will suffer as a result.

It's possible that the very fact of their mother's criminal conduct might make some people lose interest in the suffering of these children. However, in her book, Cristina Rathbone gives everyone, even a Republican Assembly member, a reason to care. Denise, one of the incarcerated mothers at MCI-Framingham whose life Rathbone followed, was convicted of a nonviolent drug offense. Denise's son was 9 years old when she was arrested. By the time she was released, he had spent five years shuttling between foster homes and his abusive father, and was, finally, in prison himself. When we visit the sins of the parents upon the children, we reap what we sow.

Periodical Bibliography

The following articles have been selected to supplement the diverse views presented in this chapter.

Phil Dirkx | "Should We Lock Up Sex Offenders and Then Throw Away the Key?" *San Luis Obispo Tribune*, July 7, 2005.

Marian W. Eldeman | "Marian W. Eldeman: Juveniles in the Adult Justice System," *Chicago Defender*, June 22, 2005.

Faith & Values Media | "Do They Deserve Dignity?" *True North*, September 22, 2002. www.truenorth.tv.

Erick Fajardo | "Build Clinics, Not Prisons, for Mentally Ill," *Daily Texan*, July 7, 2005. www.dailytexan online.com.

Thomas N. Faust | "Shifting the Responsibility of Untreated Mental Illness Out of the Criminal Justice System," *Corrections Today*, April 2003. www.aca.org.

Paige M. Harrison and Alan J. Beck | "Prison and Jail Inmates at Midyear 2004," U.S. Department of Justice, Bureau of Justice Statistics, April 2005. www.ojp.usdoj.gov/bjs.

Stephen Johnson and David B. Muhlhausen | "North American Transnational Youth Gangs: Breaking the Chain of Violence," *Backgrounder*, March 21, 2005. www.heritage.org.

Sue Mahan | "Pregnant Girls and Moms in Detention," *Justice Policy Journal: Analyzing Criminal and Juvenile Justice Issues and Policies*, Spring 2003.

Kibret Markos | "Prison Reform Idea: Make Worst Inmates Suffer," *Record*, July 3, 2005. www.northjersey. com.

Patrick McMahon | "Aging Inmates Present Prison Crisis," *USA Today*, August 11, 2003. www.globalaging.org.

Mary Beth Pfeiffer | "Prison Is Riskiest for the Sick—Patchy Treatment Causes Death, Injury for Some," *Poughkeepsie Journal*, January 5, 2003.

Steve Rayle | "History of Laws, Corrections, and the Influence of the U.S. Supreme Court on Modern Penology," *Correctional Compass*, September/October 2003. www.dc.state.fl.us.

Ed Schwartz   "The Fiscal Cost of Crime," Testimony: City
                       Council Public Safety Hearings on Prisoner
                       Reentry, February 15, 2005. www.phillyneigh
                       borhoods.org.

Megan Tady   "Warning: Must Be 18 Years Old to Execute,"
                       PopandPolitics.com, March 22, 2005. www.pop
                       andpolitics.com.

Armstrong Williams   "Much Needed Shock Treatment," *Townhall.
                       com*, June 7, 2001. www.townhall.com.

Jason Ziedenberg   "What Works to Deter Gangs?" *Detroit Free
                       Press*, April 12, 2005. www.freep.com.

For Further Discussion

Chapter 1

1. David B. Muhlhausen contends that protecting the public requires the construction of more prisons. Carolina Cordero Dyer, on the other hand, argues that public safety depends on education and employment opportunities for all Americans, and she argues that prisons undermine equal access to employment prospects for released prisoners. In your opinion, whose argument is most convincing, and why?

2. Ethan Nadelmann argues that the criminal justice system is an ineffective means of controlling drug abuse. James R. McDonough contends that drugs drive crime and that imprisoning drug criminals will make America's streets safer. Do you think that the criminalization of drug use is an effective and economical public policy? Why or why not?

Chapter 2

1. Harley G. Lappin claims that the Federal Bureau of Prisons maintains safe, secure, and cost-effective prisons. Judith Greene argues that America's prisons treat prisoners inhumanely. In your opinion, does America's prison system fairly balance security with the rights of prisoners? Explain.

2. Paul Street argues that America's prisons are racist, and that the disproportionate incarceration and disenfranchisement of people of color has a devastating effect on minority communities and on the democratic process. R.D. Davis contends that America's prisons are not racist. He argues that the reason more people of color are imprisoned is because they commit a disproportionate number of crimes. Which author makes a more convincing argument, and why?

3. Sasha Abramsky argues that America's supermax prisons are so abusive that prisoners become more violent as a result of their incarceration and upon release are more likely to be a public safety risk. Corrections professionals Thomas J. Stickrath and Gregory A. Bucholtz believe that supermax confinement is necessary to protect staff and other prisoners from the most violent offenders. They also see the existence of supermax confinement as a deterrent to prison violence. Is the potential harm of supermax confinement outweighed by its contribution to overall prison safety, in your view? What criteria should be used as a basis for deciding which prisoners go to supermax locations?

Chapter 3

1. For many critics of the prison system, the high cost to taxpayers is a primary concern. Geoffrey F. Segal argues that this expense can be significantly reduced by authorizing private companies to operate prisons. Jenni Gainsborough contends that such cost savings may come at too high a price to both staff and prisoners. What are some of the benefits of privatizing prisons mentioned by Segal? Do these benefits outweigh the risks outlined by Gainsborough? Explain.

2. Morgan Reynolds argues that prisoners should have the opportunity to work while serving time, and that private entrepreneurs should have access to prison laborers. Brandi Kishner argues that prison labor exploits prisoners and takes employment away from civilian workers outside prison. Which of these viewpoints is more convincing, in your view? Should prisoners have a choice of where and if they work while doing time? Why or why not?

3. Many jail administrators defend the practice of charging prisoners for room and board and other essentials during their imprisonment Michelle M. Sanborn argues that this practice will encourage financial responsibility on the inmates' part and save taxpayer money. Phebe Eckfeldt argues that this practice will unfairly add to the burden borne by the families of prisoners. Do you think charging prisoners for essentials is a fair solution to the rising costs of detention? Should prisoners' families be made to pay?

4. Melissa Rogers supports faith-based prison programs that provide prerelease services to prisoners in a religious context. Samantha M. Shapiro argues that "biblically based" prison programs discriminate against nonbelievers and offer special treatment to participants. In your view, should religious organizations receive tax money for conducting such programs? What are the benefits of such an arrangement? The dangers?

Chapter 4

1. James C. Backstrom argues that violent juveniles should face adult penalties in adult prisons. In contrast, Lenore Anderson calls for community-based interventions that offer juvenile offenders the chance to rehabilitate. Which approach do you think would better assure public safety? Why?

2. Rashida Edmondson argues that terminally ill prisoners who pose no public-safety threat should be allowed a compassionate release to spend their remaining days outside of prison, with family or in community care. The National Prison Hospice As-

sociation claims that the prison hospice model can effectively meet the needs of dying prisoners. According to the association, the model provides compassionate care within the prison, saving money by utilizing other prisoners to provide end-of-life care-taking tasks. List the advantages and disadvantages of each model for addressing the needs of dying patients. Which, in your opinion, is the better model?

3. Joanne Mariner argues that with somewhere between 200,000 and 400,000 mentally ill people in America's prisons, they cannot and are not receiving appropriate care by prison officials, who lack sufficient resources and training in mental health issues. Jim Doyle and Peter Fimrite contend that when the criminally mentally ill are placed in community mental health facilities, it creates a dangerous situation for both staff and patients. Community mental hospital workers, they argue, are not adequately trained to manage violent offenders. In your opinion, what are some possible solutions to this difficult dilemma?

Organizations to Contact

Aid to Children of Imprisoned Mothers, Inc. (AIM)
906 Ralph David Abernathy Blvd. SW, Atlanta, GA 30310
(404) 755-3262 • fax: (404) 755-3294
Web site: www.takingaim.net

Aid to Children of Imprisoned Mothers, Inc. is a nonprofit community-based organization that assists inmate mothers, their children and other family members in maintaining critically important family ties during the mother's incarceration. Created in 1987, AIM seeks to diminish the impact of the mother's incarceration on family relationships through a variety of support services to the children and other family members.

American Civil Liberties Union (ACLU)
National Prison Project
733 Fifteenth St. NW, Suite 620, Washington, DC 20005
(202) 393-4930 • fax: (202) 393-4931
e-mail: aclu@aclu.org • Web site: www.aclu.org

The ACLU National Prison Project seeks to create constitutional conditions of confinement and strengthen prisoners' rights through class action litigation and public education. Policy priorities include reducing prison overcrowding, improving prisoner medical care, eliminating violence and maltreatment in prisons and jails, and minimizing the reliance on incarceration as a criminal justice sanction. Publications include the *National Prison Project Journal*, the *Prisoners Assistance Directory*, and various other reports.

American Correctional Association (ACA)
4380 Forbes Blvd., Lanham, MD 20706-4322
(301) 918-1800 • (800)-ACA-JOIN
e-mail: jeffw@aca.org • Web site: www.aca.org

The ACA is the oldest and largest correctional association in the world. It is committed to improving national and international correctional policy and to promoting the professional development of those working in the field of corrections. The ACA offers a variety of books and correspondence courses on corrections and criminal justice and publishes the bimonthly magazine *Corrections Today*.

Books Not Bars
Ella Baker Center for Human Rights
344 Fortieth St., Oakland, CA 94609
(510) 428-3939 • fax: (510) 428-3940
Web site: www.ellabakercenter.org

Books Not Bars, a project of the Ella Baker Center for Human Rights, works to reallocate public resources away from punishment and toward opportunity for young people, to restore communities, and to redesign the criminal justice system. Books Not Bars believes that the fundamental goal of the criminal justice system should be restoration and reconciliation.

Building Blocks for Youth
Youth Law Center
1010 Vermont Ave. NW, Suite 310, Washington, DC 20005
(202) 637-0377 • fax: (202) 379-1600
e-mail: info.bby@erols.com
Web site: www.buildingblocksforyouth.org
The Building Blocks for Youth initiative is an alliance of children and youth advocates, researchers, law enforcement professionals, and community organizers that seeks to reduce what it sees as the overrepresentation and disparate treatment of youth of color in the justice system, and promote fair, rational, and effective juvenile justice policies.

Bureau of Prisons
320 First St. NW, Washington, DC 20534
(202) 307-3198
e-mail: info@bop.gov • Web site: www.bop.gov
The Federal Bureau of Prisons was established in 1930. The mission of the bureau is to provide humane care for federal inmates, to professionalize the prison service, and to ensure consistent and centralized administration of the more than 106 institutions, six regional offices, central office (headquarters), two staff training centers, and twenty-eight community corrections offices. The bureau protects public safety by ensuring that federal offenders serve their sentences in facilities that are safe, humane, cost-efficient, and appropriately secure. The bureau publishes the book *The State of the Bureau*.

Citizens United for the Rehabilitation of Errants (CURE)
PO Box 2310, National Capitol Station, Washington, DC 20013-2310
(202) 789-2126
e-mail: dccure@curenational.org
Web site: www.curenational.org
CURE is a nationwide membership organization of families of prisoners, prisoners, former prisoners, and other concerned citizens dedicated to reducing crime through reform of the criminal justice system. CURE's goals are to use prisons only for those who

have to be in them and to provide prisoners all the rehabilitative opportunities they need to turn their lives around.

Commission on Safety and Abuse in America's Prisons

601 Thirteenth St. NW, Suite 1150 South, Washington, DC 20005
(202) 637-6355 • fax: (202) 639-6066
e-mail: info@prisoncommission.org
Web site: www.prisoncommission.org

The Commission on Safety and Abuse in America's Prisons is a diverse, nonpartisan panel that formed in March 2005 to explore the most serious problems inside U.S. correctional facilities and their impact on the incarcerated, the men and women who staff facilities, and society at large. The commission is facilitating a national dialogue about the most serious problems associated with life behind bars and seeking constructive recommendations for reform. The commission will recommend strategies for operating correctional facilities that more closely reflect America's values and serve America's best interests.

Critical Resistance

National Office
1904 Franklin St., Suite 504, Oakland, CA 94612
(510) 444-0484
e-mail: crnational@criticalresistance.org
Web site: www.criticalresistance.org

Critical Resistance is a national, grassroots, member-based organization working to build an international movement to end the prison industrial complex by challenging the belief that incarcerating people makes communities safer.

Families Against Mandatory Minimums (FAMM)

1612 K St. NW, Suite 1400, Washington, DC 20006
(202) 822-6704
e-mail: famm@famm.org • Web site: www.famm.org

FAMM is a national advocacy group that works to repeal mandatory minimum sentences by publicizing cases that dramatize what it sees as the unfairness of these laws. FAMM produces a bimonthly newsletter, *FAMMgram*.

Federal Prison Policy Project (FPPP)

PO Box 742552, Riverdale, GA 30274
(770) 477-9814
e-mail: info@fppp.org • Web site: www.fppp.org

The mission of the Federal Prison Policy Project is to return responsible justice to the judicial system and to seek revision of the current laws by educating the public and examining programs for submission to officials and congressional leaders to achieve changes for a fair and just system.

Heartland Institute
19 South LaSalle St., Suite 903, Chicago, IL 60603
(312) 377-4000
e-mail: think@heartland.org • Web site: www.heartland.org

The Heartland Institute is an independent, nonprofit source of research and commentary founded in Chicago, Illinois, in 1984. It is not affiliated with any political party, business, or foundation. It seeks to empower people with ideas based on the principles of individual rights and limited government.

The Heritage Foundation
214 Massachusetts Ave. NE, Washington, DC 20002-4999
(202) 546-4400 • fax: (202) 546-8328
e-mail: info@heritage.org • Web site: www.heritage.org

The Heritage Foundation is a research and educational institute founded in 1973. The mission of the foundation is to formulate and promote conservative public policies based on the principles of free enterprise, limited government, individual freedom, traditional American values, and a strong national defense.

Justice Policy Institute (JPI)
1003 K St. NW, Suite 500, Washington, DC 20001
(202) 558-7974 • fax: (202) 558-7978
e-mail: info@justicepolicy.org • Web site: www.justicepolicy.org

The Justice Policy Institute is a nonprofit research and public policy organization dedicated to ending society's reliance on incarceration and promoting effective and just solutions to social problems. Since 1996, JPI has been a voice for crafting workable solutions to age-old problems plaguing America's juvenile and criminal justice systems.

Law Enforcement Alliance of America (LEAA)
7700 Leesburg Pike, Suite 421, Falls Church, VA 22043
(703) 847-2677 • fax: (703) 556-6485
e-mail: editor@leaa.org • Web site: www.leaa.org

The Law Enforcement Alliance of America is the nation's largest nonprofit, nonpartisan coalition of law enforcement professionals, crime victims, and concerned citizens united for justice. With a major focus on public education, LEAA is dedicated to providing hard facts and real-world insights into the world of law enforcement and the battle against violent crime. LEAA fights at every level of government for legislation that reduces violent crime while preserving the rights of honest citizens, particularly the right of self-defense. It publishes the quarterly magazine *LEAA Advocate*, which periodically addresses correctional issues, and *Shield* magazine, to educate citizens on the realities of criminal violence.

National Institute of Justice (NIJ)
810 Seventh St. NW, Washington, DC 20531
(202) 307-2942 • fax: (202) 307-6394
Web site: www.ojp.usdoj.gov

The National Institute of Justice is the research, development, and evaluation agency of the U.S. Department of Justice and is dedicated to researching crime control and justice issues. The NIJ's mission is to advance scientific research to enhance the administration of justice and public safety.

November Coalition
282 West Astor, Colville, WA 99114
(509) 684-1550
e-mail: moreinfo@november.org Web • site: www.november.org

The November Coalition is a nonprofit grassroots organization with a mission to raise awareness in individuals and communities about existing and impending dangers of what it sees as an overly powerful federal government acting beyond constitutional constraints. The November Coalition works to end drug war injustice and calls for a return to parole for federal prisoners.

Prisons Foundation
1718 M St. NW, #151, Washington, DC 20036
(202) 393-1511 • fax: (727) 538-2095
e-mail: staff@prisonsfoundation.org
Web site: www.prisonsfoundation.org

The Prisons Foundation is a nonprofit organization dedicated to promoting education and the arts behind bars and alternatives to incarceration.

RAND Corporation
1700 Main St., Santa Monica, CA 90407-2138
(310) 393-0411 • fax: (310) 393-4818
e-mail: correspondence@rand.org • Web site: www.rand.org

The RAND Corporation is a nonprofit research organization providing analysis and effective solutions that address the challenges facing the public and private sectors around the world. The RAND Corporation publishes a wide variety of reports, including information on criminal justice issues and drug policy.

Vera Institute of Justice

233 Broadway, Twelfth Floor, New York, NY 10279
(212) 334-1300 • fax: (212) 941-9407
e-mail: contactvera@vera.org • Web site: www.vera.org

The Vera Institute of Justice is a nonprofit organization that works closely with leaders in government and civil society to improve the services people rely on for safety and justice. Vera develops programs that often grow into self-sustaining organizations, studies social problems and current responses, and provides advice and assistance to government officials in New York and around the world.

Bibliography of Books

Sasha Abramsky   *Hard Time Blues: How Politics Built a Prison Nation.* New York: Thomas Dunne Books, 2002.

Ronald H. Aday   *Aging Prisoners: Crises in American Corrections.* Westport, CT: Praeger, 2002.

Dana M. Britton   *At Work in the Iron Cage: The Prison as Gendered Organization.* New York: New York University Press, 2003.

James H. Burton   *The Big House: Life Inside a Supermax Security Prison.* Stillwater, MN: Voyageur Press, 2004.

Kerry Carrington and Russell Hogg, eds.   *Critical Criminology: Issues, Debates, Challenges.* Portland, OR: Willan, 2002.

Meda Chesney-Lind and Lisa Pasko, eds.   *Girls, Women, and Crime: Selected Readings.* Thousand Oaks, CA: Sage, 2004.

Andrew Coyle, Allison Campbell, and Rodney Neufeld, eds.,   *Capitalist Punishment: Prison Privatization and Human Rights.* Atlanta: Clarity Press, 2003.

Angela Davis   *Are Prisons Obsolete?* New York: Seven Stories Press, 2003.

David R. Dow   *Executed on a Technicality: Lethal Injustice on America's Death Row.* New York: Beacon Press, 2005.

Mark Dow   *American Gulag: Inside U.S. Immigration Prisons.* Berkeley: University of California Press, 2004.

Alan Elsner   *Gates of Injustice: The Crisis in America's Prisons.* Princeton, NJ: Prentice Hall, 2004.

David Farabee   *Rethinking Rehabilitation: Why Can't We Reform Our Criminals.* Washington DC: AEI Press, 2005.

Joseph T. Hallinan   *Going up the River: Travels in a Prison Nation.* New York: Random House, 2001.

Gene Healy, ed.   *Go Directly to Jail: The Criminalization of Almost Everything.* Washington, DC: Cato Institute, 2004.

Michael Jacobson   *How to Reduce Crime and End Mass Incarceration.* New York: New York University Press, 2005.

David R. Karp and Todd R. Clear, eds.   *What Is Community Justice?* Thousand Oaks, CA: Sage, 2002.

Roslyn Muraskin, ed.   *Key Correctional Issues.* Upper Saddle River, NJ: Pearson/Prentice Hall, 2005.

David L. Myers — *Boys Among Men: Trying and Sentencing Juveniles as Adults.* Westport, CT: Praeger, 2005.

Donice Neal, ed. — *Supermax Prisons: Beyond the Rock.* Lanham, MD: American Correctional Association, 2003.

Joycelyn M. Pollock — *Prisons and Prison Life: Costs and Consequences.* Los Angeles: Roxbury, 2004.

Prisons Foundation — *Prisons Almanac 2005.* Washington, DC: Prisons Foundation, 2005.

Lorna Rhodes — *Total Confinement: Madness and Reason in the Maximum Security Prison.* Berkeley: University of California Press, 2004.

Thane Rosenbaum — *The Myth of Moral Justice, Why Our Legal System Fails to Do What's Right.* New York: HarperCollins, 2004.

Henry Ruth and Kevin R. Reitz — *The Challenge of Crime: Rethinking Our Response.* Cambridge, MA: Harvard University Press, 2003.

Vincent Schiraldi and Jason Ziedenberg — *Cellblocks or Classrooms: The Funding of Higher Education and Corrections and Its Impact on African American Men.* Washington, DC: Justice Policy Institute, 2002.

Pamela J. Schram and Barbara Koons-Witt, eds. — *Gendered (In)Justice: Theory and Practice in Feminist Criminology.* Long Grove, IL: Waveland Press, 2004.

Randall G. Shelden and William B. Brown — *Criminal Justice in America: A Critical View.* Boston: Allyn and Bacon, 2003.

Stephen Stanko, Wayne Gillespie, and Gordon A. Crews — *Living in Prison: A History of the Correctional System with an Insider's View.* Westport, CT: Greenwood Press, 2004.

Julia Sudbury — *Global Lockdown: Race, Gender, and the Prison-Industrial Complex.* New York: Routledge, 2004.

Alexander Tabarrok, ed. — *Changing the Guard: Private Prisons and the Control of Crime.* Oakland, CA: Independent Institute, 2003.

Jeremy Travis and Michelle Waul, eds. — *Prisoners Once Removed: The Impact of Incarceration and Reentry on Children, Families, and Communities.* Washington, DC: Urban Institute Press, 2003.

Index